Field Guides to Finding a New Career

Real Estate

The Field Guides to Finding a New Career series

Field Guides to Finding a New Career

Real Estate

By Rowan Riley

Ferguson Publishing
An imprint of Infobase Publishing

Field Guides to Finding a New Career: Real Estate

Ferguson
An imprint of Infobase Publishing
132 West 31st Street
New York, NY 10001

Library of Congress Cataloging-in-Publication Data

Riley, Rowan.
    Real estate / by Rowan Riley.
        p. cm. — (Field guides to finding a new career)
    Includes bibliographical references and index.
    ISBN-13: 978-0-8160-7995-7 (hardcover : alk. paper)
    ISBN-10: 0-8160-7995-1 (hardcover : alk. paper) 1. Real estate business—
Vocational guidance—United States. I. Title.
    HD1375.R485 2010
    333.33023'73—dc22

                                                                    2010013961

Ferguson books are available at special discounts when purchased in bulk quantities for businesses, associations, institutions, or sales promotions. Please call our Special Sales Department in New York at (212) 967-8800 or (800) 322-8755.

You can find Ferguson on the World Wide Web at http://www.fergpubco.com

Produced by Print Matters, Inc.
Text design by A Good Thing, Inc.
Illustrations by Molly Crabapple
Cover design by Takeshi Takahashi
Cover printed by Bang Printing, Brainerd, MN
Book printed and bound by Bang Printing, Brainerd, MN
Date printed: June 2010

Printed in the United States of America

10 9 8 7 6 5 4 3 2 1

This book is printed on acid-free paper.

Contents

Introduction: Finding a New Career

Today, changing jobs is an accepted and normal part of life. In fact, according to the Bureau of Labor Statistics, Americans born between 1957 and 1964 held an average of 9.6 jobs from the ages of 18 to 36. The reasons for this are varied: To begin with, people live longer and healthier lives than they did in the past and accordingly have more years of active work life. However, the economy of the twenty-first century is in a state of constant and rapid change, and the workforce of the past does not always meet the needs of the future. Furthermore, fewer and fewer industries provide bonuses such as pensions and retirement health plans, which provide an incentive for staying with the same firm. Other workers experience epiphanies, spiritual growth, or various sorts of personal challenges that lead them to question the paths they have chosen.

Job instability is another prominent factor in the modern workplace. In the last five years, the United States has lost 2.6 *million jobs*; in 2005 alone, 370,000 workers were affected by mass layoffs. Moreover, because of new technology, changing labor markets, ageism, and a host of other factors, many educated, experienced professionals and skilled blue-collar workers have difficulty finding jobs in their former career tracks. Finally—and not just for women—the realities of juggling work and family life, coupled with economic necessity, often force radical revisions of career plans.

No matter how normal or accepted changing careers might be, however, the time of transition can also be a time of anxiety. Faced with the necessity of changing direction in the middle of their journey through life, many find themselves lost. Many career-changers find themselves asking questions such as: Where do I want to go from here? How do I get there? How do I prepare myself for the journey? Thankfully, the Field Guides to Finding a New Career are here to show the way. Using the language and visual style of a travel guide, we show you that reorienting yourself and reapplying your skills and knowledge to a new career is not an uphill slog, but an exciting journey of exploration. No matter whether you are in your twenties or close to retirement age, you can bravely set out to explore new paths and discover new vistas.

Though this series forms an organic whole, each volume is also designed to be a comprehensive, stand-alone, all-in-one guide to getting motivated, getting back on your feet, and getting back to work. We thoroughly discuss common issues such as going back to school, managing your household finances, putting your old skills to work in new situations, and selling yourself to potential employers. Each volume focuses on a broad career field, roughly grouped by Bureau of Labor Statistics' career clusters. Each chapter will focus on a particular career, suggesting new career paths suitable for an individual with that experience and training as well as practical issues involved in seeking and applying for a position.

Many times, the first question career-changers ask is, "Is this new path right for me?" Our self-assessment quiz, coupled with the career compasses at the beginning of each chapter, will help you to match your personal attributes to set you on the right track. Do you possess a storehouse of skilled knowledge? Are you the sort of person who puts others before yourself? Are you methodical and organized? Do you communicate effectively and clearly? Are you good at math? And how do you react to stress? All of these qualities contribute to career success—but they are not equally important in all jobs.

Many career-changers find working for themselves to be more hassle-free and rewarding than working for someone else. However, going at it alone, whether as a self-employed individual or a small-business owner, provides its own special set of challenges. Appendix A, "Going Solo: Starting Your Own Business," is designed to provide answers to many common questions and solutions to everyday problems, from income taxes to accounting to providing health insurance for yourself and your family.

For those who choose to work for someone else, how do you find a job, particularly when you have been out of the labor market for a while? Appendix B, "Outfitting Yourself for Career Success," is designed to answer these questions. It provides not only advice on résumé and self-presentation, but also the latest developments in looking for jobs, such as online resources, headhunters, and placement agencies. Additionally, it recommends how to explain an absence from the workforce to a potential employer.

Changing careers can be stressful, but it can also be a time of exciting personal growth and discovery. We hope that the Field Guides to Finding a New Career not only help you get your bearings in today's employment jungle, but set you on the path to personal fulfillment, happiness, and prosperity.

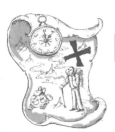

How to Use This Book

Career Compasses

Each chapter begins with a series of "career compasses" to help you get your bearings and determine if this job is right for you, based on your answers to the self-assessment quiz at the beginning of the book. Does it require a mathematical mindset? Communication skills? Organizational skills? If you're not a "people person," a job requiring you to interact with the public might not be right for you. On the other hand, your organizational skills might be just what are needed in the back office.

Destination

A brief overview, giving you an introduction to the career, briefly explaining what it is, its advantages, why it is so satisfying, its growth potential, and its income potential.

You Are Here

A self-assessment asking you to locate yourself on your journey. Are you working in a related field? Are you working in a field where some skills will transfer? Or are you doing something completely different? In each case, we suggest ways to reapply your skills, gain new ones, and launch yourself on your new career path.

Navigating the Terrain

To help you on your way, we have provided a handy map showing the stages in your journey to a new career. "Navigating the Terrain" will show you the road you need to follow to get where you are going. Since the answers are not the same for everyone and every career, we are sure to show how there are multiple ways to get to the same destination.

Organizing Your Expedition

Fleshing out "Navigating the Terrain," we give explicit directions on how to enter this new career: Decide on a destination, scout the terrain, and decide on a path that is right for you. Of course, the answers are not the same for everyone.

Landmarks

People have different needs at different ages. "Landmarks" presents advice specific to the concerns of each age demographic: early career (twenties), mid-career (thirties to forties), senior employees (fifties) and second-career starters (sixties). We address not only issues such as overcoming age discrimination, but also possible concerns of spouses and families (for instance, paying college tuition with reduced income) and keeping up with new technologies.

Essential Gear

Indispensable tips for career-changers on things such as gearing your résumé to a job in a new field, finding contacts and networking, obtaining further education and training, and how to gain experience in the new field.

Notes from the Field

Sometimes it is useful to consult with those who have gone before for insights and advice. "Notes from the Field" presents interviews with career-changers, presenting motivations and methods that you can identify with.

Further Resources

Finally, we give a list of "expedition outfitters" to provide you with further resources and trade resources.

Make the Most of Your Journey

The real estate market is a subject that will always fascinate and frustrate Americans. We are all curious about real estate on some level, even if it is just a casual interest, as in, "Did you see that beautiful brownstone for sale at the end of the block?" or, "Did you hear how much Mel Gibson paid for his new home?" In a normal economy, real estate is an important asset that provides stable cash flow plus appreciation over time. However, in the past few years, the real estate market has been shattered and fractured due to the greed and avarice of several large lending corporations. Nathanial Hawthorne once said, "What we call real estate—the solid ground to build a house on—is the broad foundation on which nearly all the guilt of this world rests."

Our economy may still be feeling the effects of the sub-prime mortgage crisis for many years to come, but it is important to remember that real estate—and in a broader sense, land ownership—is what this country was founded on. It is the reason why the Pilgrims originally came to America and why so many people moved West. America's real estate industry was founded by a group of pioneers who risked their lives in search of profitable land just beyond the horizon, so it is not surprising that many of the people in today's real estate industry are entrepreneurial in spirit. What this country needs now more so than ever is a new generation of honest and visionary professionals who can revitalize the real estate industry and reform its lending policies and environmental practices.

The nine professions profiled in this volume expose you to a wide variety of fields within the real estate industry, but they do not encompass all the careers available. Despite the corruption and scandal that has surrounded the real estate industry since 2007, the industry continues to grow. The green movement in particular has given rise to a lot of new and exciting career opportunities, some of which are described in this volume. All of the careers mentioned offer diverse work environments where one is exposed to a wide variety of people and settings. However, if you are a self-motivated and entrepreneurial person who is eager to leave a personal mark in the real estate industry, this volume offers several careers to satisfy all your Herculian ambitions.

Take, for instance, urban planners—the ground troops of the real estate industry. Urban planners examine blueprints for local parks by day, and do battle against corrupt politicians and special interest parties by night. Their job is to improve the functioning of cities and towns by creating infrastructure, conserving land, improving transportation systems, and revitalizing rundown areas. Planners meet with politicians, citizens, and special interest parties to hear their needs and also to get their own plans approved. As Mark Pelligrini, director of urban planning in Manchester, Connecticut, put it, "Planners need to plan *with* people and not *for* people."

If you like the sound of urban planning but would prefer to work independently, building inspection is an interesting and important line of work. Building inspectors travel to a variety of different buildings, homes, and construction sites to make sure they comply with safety regulations and building codes. It is important work that requires keen observation and a thorough understanding of plumbing, maintenance, and other construction trades. If the inspector finds that a building is in violation of one of the codes, he or she has the right to shutter the building or suspend construction. In many respects, building inspectors are the whistleblowers of the real estate industry.

A closely related profession to that of inspector is real estate appraiser. Appraisers also examine properties and have a similar understanding of the construction trades; only instead of working for the government, which most building inspectors do, appraisers are often self-employed. Starting an appraisal company does not require a lot of overhead, so it is great for those who are interested in architecture or construction and want to start their own business.

We are all familiar with the job of real estate agents, but in recent years the career has evolved thanks to the advent of the Internet. Agents can now market themselves with greater focus and are able to cater to niche markets, such as ranch and farm, out-of-state clients, or high-end properties. After a few years at an established agency, many agents leave to start their own agencies. Alternatively, agencies are a great jumping off point if you would rather move onto a different field. This is particularly true for those interested in brokering, property management, or real estate investment.

Investing in real estate and becoming a landlord is another excellent entry into the real estate industry. If you make the right investment and find the right tenant, you can make a tidy profit from being a landlord. More importantly, you learn how to invest in and care for a property, which you can apply to virtually any real estate profession. Landlords are often mislabeled as individuals whose sole concern is getting your rent check on time. While it is true that the age-old practice of leasing land sometimes feels like it is stuck in medieval times, in the past few decades a slew of tenant laws have been passed and leasing procedures have become more regulated. It also seems as though landlords are beginning to realize that protecting their property also means protecting their tenants.

If you do not have the money to invest in a property but want to eventually become a landlord, a good way to gain practice is to take a job as a property manager. Commercial property managers handle the maintenance, security, and financial operations for a variety of properties, ranging from skyscrapers to one-story restaurants. There are also residential managers who live rent-free in the buildings they manage. There are very few, if any, requirements for becoming a single unit property manager, and it is an excellent way to learn how to maintain a building.

Developers are the most powerful people in today's real estate market, which can also make them the most dangerous. Developers are primarily known for mass-producing buildings and tract homes with little or no craftsmanship, but in recent years developers are making an effort to customize their properties and specialize in green designs. As a developer, you have the potential to make a lot of money, but without the proper knowledge and experience, you can go bankrupt faster than Donald Trump can say "You're fired." There is a tremendous amount of risk involved in the job. Self-employed developers or those who own small businesses often lose their financing, and even at the corporate level a developer's earnings depend on unpredictable factors, such as geographic trends and the condition of the economy.

Those who are a bit too cautious or risk-adverse to become developers might want to consider entering the risk-management business. Developers, investment firms, and banks often rely on real estate financial analysts to calculate the risks and potential returns of certain real estate investments. If you like crunching numbers and do not mind sitting at a desk for most of the day, real estate analysis is engaging work that pays well. Those with a background in accounting or finance should be able to break into the field quite easily.

If you are looking for the antithesis of a desk job, look no further than the building profession. Building has become somewhat of a dying art thanks to developers out-pricing all the competition, but there are still those who prefer a builder's solid craftsmanship to a developer's prefabricated components. Builders not only work with their hands—they also work with architects, contractors, plumbers, construction workers, and many more experienced tradesmen. It is an incredibly active job that can be exhausting at times, but most builders enjoy the craft too much to complain. That age-old adage—choose a career that you love, and you will never have to work a day in your life—really seems to apply to this particular occupation.

Warren Buffett once said, "In business, the rearview mirror is always cleaner than the windshield." Before you embark on a career in real estate, take a moment to look in the rearview mirror and reflect on the events that led to the recent real estate crisis. Learn from the missteps that created such a widespread economic downturn. Internalize this knowledge, and soon you will be able to put the car in drive and head toward a bright new career path in this most dynamic and relevant field.

Self-Assessment Quiz

I: Relevant Knowledge

1. How many years of specialized training have you had?
   (a) None, it is not required
   (b) Several weeks to several months of training
   (c) A year-long course or other preparation
   (d) Years of preparation in graduate or professional school, or equivalent job experience

2. Would you consider training to obtain certification or other required credentials?
   (a) No
   (b) Yes, but only if it is legally mandated
   (c) Yes, but only if it is the industry standard
   (d) Yes, if it is helpful (even if not mandatory)

3. In terms of achieving success, how would you rate the following qualities in order from least to most important?
   (a) ability, effort, preparation
   (b) ability, preparation, effort
   (c) preparation, ability, effort
   (d) preparation, effort, ability

4. How would you feel about keeping track of current developments in your field?
   (a) I prefer a field where very little changes
   (b) If there were a trade publication, I would like to keep current with that
   (c) I would be willing to regularly recertify my credentials or learn new systems
   (d) I would be willing to aggressively keep myself up-to-date in a field that changes constantly

5. For whatever reason, you have to train a bright young successor to do your job. How quickly will he or she pick it up?
    (a) Very quickly
    (b) He or she can pick up the necessary skills on the job
    (c) With the necessary training he or she should succeed with hard work and concentration
    (d) There is going to be a long breaking-in period—there is no substitute for experience

II: Caring

1. How would you react to the following statement: "Other people are the most important thing in the world?"
    (a) No! Me first!
    (b) I do not really like other people, but I do make time for them
    (c) Yes, but you have to look out for yourself first
    (d) Yes, to such a degree that I often neglect my own well-being

2. Who of the following is the best role model?
    (a) Ayn Rand
    (b) Napoléon Bonaparte
    (c) Bill Gates
    (d) Florence Nightingale

3. How do you feel about pets?
    (a) I do not like animals at all
    (b) Dogs and cats and such are OK, but not for me
    (c) I have a pet, or I wish I did
    (d) I have several pets, and caring for them occupies significant amounts of my time

4. Which of the following sets of professions seems most appealing to you?
    (a) business leader, lawyer, entrepreneur
    (b) politician, police officer, athletic coach
    (c) teacher, religious leader, counselor
    (d) nurse, firefighter, paramedic

5. How well would you have to know someone to give them $100 in a harsh but not life-threatening circumstance? It would have to be...
    (a) ...a close family member or friend (brother or sister, best friend)
    (b) ...a more distant friend or relation (second cousin, coworkers)
    (c) ...an acquaintance (a coworker, someone from a community organization or church)
    (d) ...a complete stranger

III: Organizational Skills

1. Do you create sub-folders to further categorize the items in your "Pictures" and "Documents" folders on your computer?
    (a) No
    (b) Yes, but I do not use them consistently
    (c) Yes, and I use them consistently
    (d) Yes, and I also do so with my e-mail and music library

2. How do you keep track of your personal finances?
    (a) I do not, and I am never quite sure how much money is in my checking account
    (b) I do not really, but I always check my online banking to make sure I have money
    (c) I am generally very good about budgeting and keeping track of my expenses, but sometimes I make mistakes
    (d) I do things such as meticulously balance my checkbook, fill out Excel spreadsheets of my monthly expenses, and file my receipts

3. Do you systematically order commonly used items in your kitchen?
    (a) My kitchen is a mess
    (b) I can generally find things when I need them
    (c) A place for everything, and everything in its place
    (d) Yes, I rigorously order my kitchen and do things like alphabetize spices and herbal teas

4. How do you do your laundry?
    (a) I cram it in any old way
    (b) I separate whites and colors

    (c)   I separate whites and colors, plus whether it gets dried

    (d)   Not only do I separate whites and colors and drying or non-drying, I organize things by type of clothes or some other system

5.   Can you work in clutter?

    (a)   Yes, in fact I feel energized by the mess

    (b)   A little clutter never hurt anyone

    (c)   No, it drives me insane

    (d)   Not only does my workspace need to be neat, so does that of everyone around me

IV: Communication Skills

1.   Do people ask you to speak up, not mumble, or repeat yourself?

    (a)   All the time

    (b)   Often

    (c)   Sometimes

    (d)   Never

2.   How do you feel about speaking in public?

    (a)   It terrifies me

    (b)   I can give a speech or presentation if I have to, but it is awkward

    (c)   No problem!

    (d)   I frequently give lectures and addresses, and I am very good at it

3.   What's the difference between *their, they're,* and *there*?

    (a)   I do not know

    (b)   I know there is a difference, but I make mistakes in usage

    (c)   I know the difference, but I cannot articulate it

    (d)   *Their* is the third-person possessive, *they're* is a contraction for *they are,* and *there is* a deictic adverb meaning "in that place"

4.   Do you avoid writing long letters or e-mails because you are ashamed of your spelling, punctuation, and grammatical mistakes?

    (a)   Yes

    (b)   Yes, but I am either trying to improve or just do not care what people think

(c)   The few mistakes I make are easily overlooked

(d)   Save for the occasional typo, I do not ever make mistakes in usage

5.   Which choice best characterizes the most challenging book you are willing to read in your spare time?

(a)   I do not read

(b)   Light fiction reading such as the Harry Potter series, *The Da Vinci Code*, or mass-market paperbacks

(c)   Literary fiction or mass-market nonfiction such as history or biography

(d)   Long treatises on technical, academic, or scientific subjects

V: Mathematical Skills

1.   Do spreadsheets make you nervous?

(a)   Yes, and I do not use them at all

(b)   I can perform some simple tasks, but I feel that I should leave them to people who are better-qualified than myself

(c)   I feel that I am a better-than-average spreadsheet user

(d)   My job requires that I be very proficient with them

2.   What is the highest level math class you have ever taken?

(a)   I flunked high-school algebra

(b)   Trigonometry or pre-calculus

(c)   College calculus or statistics

(d)   Advanced college mathematics

3.   Would you rather make a presentation in words or using numbers and figures?

(a)   Definitely in words

(b)   In words, but I could throw in some simple figures and statistics if I had to

(c)   I could strike a balance between the two

(d)   Using numbers as much as possible; they are much more precise

4.   Cover the answers below with a sheet of paper, and then solve the following word problem: Mary has been legally able to vote for exactly half her life. Her husband John is three years older than she. Next year,

their son Harvey will be exactly one-quarter of John's age. How old was Mary when Harvey was born?
(a) I couldn't work out the answer
(b) 25
(c) 26
(d) 27

5. Cover the answers below with a sheet of paper, and then solve the following word problem: There are seven children on a school bus. Each child has seven book bags. Each bag has seven big cats in it. Each cat has seven kittens. How many legs are there on the bus?
(a) I couldn't work out the answer
(b) 2,415
(c) 16,821
(d) 10,990

VI: Ability to Manage Stress

1. It is the end of the working day, you have 20 minutes to finish an hour-long job, and you are scheduled to pick up your children. Your supervisor asks you why you are not finished. You:
(a) Have a panic attack
(b) Frantically redouble your efforts
(c) Calmly tell her you need more time, make arrangements to have someone else pick up the kids, and work on the project past closing time
(d) Calmly tell her that you need more time to do it right and that you have to leave, or ask if you can release this flawed version tonight

2. When you are stressed, do you tend to:
(a) Feel helpless, develop tightness in your chest, break out in cold sweats, or have other extreme, debilitating physiological symptoms?
(b) Get irritable and develop a hair-trigger temper, drink too much, obsess over the problem, or exhibit other "normal" signs of stress?
(c) Try to relax, keep your cool, and act as if there is no problem
(d) Take deep, cleansing breaths and actively try to overcome the feelings of stress

3. The last time I was so angry or frazzled that I lost my composure was:
    (a) Last week or more recently
    (b) Last month
    (c) Over a year ago
    (d) So long ago I cannot remember

4. Which of the following describes you?
    (a) Stress is a major disruption in my life, people have spoken to me about my anger management issues, or I am on medication for my anxiety and stress
    (b) I get anxious and stressed out easily
    (c) Sometimes life can be a challenge, but you have to climb that mountain!
    (d) I am generally easygoing

5. What is your ideal vacation?
    (a) I do not take vacations; I feel my work life is too demanding
    (b) I would just like to be alone, with no one bothering me
    (c) I would like to do something not too demanding, like a cruise, with friends and family
    (d) I am an adventurer; I want to do exciting (or even dangerous) things and visit foreign lands

Scoring:

For each category...

For every answer of *a*, add zero points to your score.
For every answer of *b*, add ten points to your score.
For every answer of *c*, add fifteen points to your score.
For every answer of *d*, add twenty points to your score.

The result is your percentage in that category.

Real Estate Agent

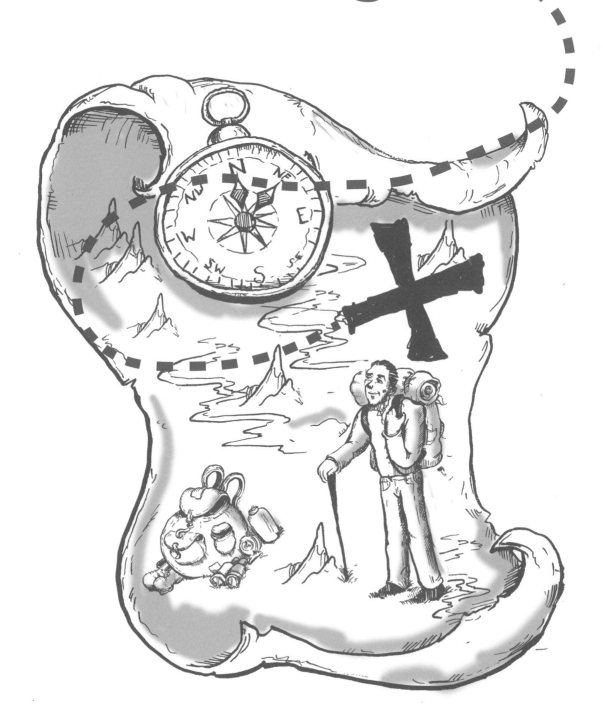

Real Estate Agent

Career Compasses

Get your bearings on what it takes to become a real estate agent.

Relevant Knowledge of a particular region's real estate market, including local zoning and tax laws (40%)

Communication Skills for building client relations and sealing the deal on a sale (30%)

Ability to Manage Stress during tense negotiations, big deals, or when the real estate market is in decline (20%)

Mathematical Skills when arranging the financing on a home or during price negotiations with buyers and sellers (10%)

Destination: Real Estate Agent

Having a plot of land to call our own is the American dream. Yet oftentimes we get so caught up in the fantasy of owning a dream home that we forget how much time, stress, and financial risk is involved in making the purchase. It is a real estate agent's job to navigate us through the nation's complex and often unpredictable real estate market.

During real estate transactions, an agent acts as an intermediary between the buyer and seller. This may sound straightforward, but the job entails far more than just sales expertise. Real estate agents need to know everything about a particular region's real estate market, including local zoning and tax laws. In addition, agents must have a good understanding of home financing because in this day and age most people cannot afford a home without taking out a mortgage.

Agents put a lot of effort into obtaining listings, which are written agreements that authorize sellers to place properties for sale with an agency. Once a home is listed, agents research similar homes in the area to determine a competitive market price for the property. From there, an agent can start marketing properties by placing ads in local papers, sticking "for sale" signs in the ground, and entering the property into a multiple listing service (MLS), which is a database that enables agents to share information about their properties with other agents.

Essential Gear

Keep an eye on the economic climate. The real estate market changes rapidly and is susceptible to economic decline, so agents should have a good feel for economics. It also helps to have a keen eye for real estate trends—those abandoned factories on the edge of town could one day be converted into high-end lofts.

Although agents typically represent sellers on an exclusive basis, they also represent buyers, but mostly on a nonexclusive basis. Buying a home is one of the largest investments people make in their lifetime, so it is important for agents to have a good sense of the buyer's finances and personal needs. Does the buyer need to be near a good school district? Or is the floor plan more important? A good agent asks the buyer these types of questions before showing properties.

Once the buyer finds a home, price negotiations begin between the buyer and seller. This is usually the most exciting—albeit stressful—part of an agent's job. Negotiating the sale of a home is not unlike playing a game of high-stakes poker. You never really know how much the buyer or seller is willing to stake, but a good agent can tell when it is appropriate to make a counteroffer and when it is time to settle. Timing is also essential. Agents should be able to put together an offer overnight and set up a loan within a matter of weeks.

In return for bringing the buyer and seller together and closing the sale, the agent receives a percentage of the amount that the buyer pays for the property. In addition, the agent who obtained the listing for the property also receives a commission. An agent's commission differs depending on their experience level and where they work. Most agents sell residential properties. However, a small number—usually employed in large firms—sell commercial, industrial, or other types of real estate. These jobs require you to have knowledge in a specific field.

Regardless of where you work, real estate can be a tough industry to break into. As a real estate agent, you face intense competition from more experienced agents, and you are working on commission so there is no guarantee of a paycheck. That said, the job is not without its perks. Agents work on a contract basis, which means that they can make their own schedule and even work part-time or from home. In addition, there are many opportunities for advancement in real estate. Agents working at large firms are often promoted to sales manager or general manager, while those at smaller firms often opt to take the broker's license and start their own business.

Essential Gear

Use technology to your advantage. Most real estate agents are on the computer every day, e-mailing clients about open houses or researching properties in the area. If you are interested in becoming an agent, you should be comfortable with computers and have a working understanding of how agents utilize technology. For example, agents rely heavily on the Internet for marketing purposes, so you should familiarize yourself with marketing tools such as the Multiple Listings Service (MLS).

If real estate sounds like the job for you, then you will be pleased to know that it does not take much training or experience to become a licensed real estate agent. If you paused after reading the word *licensed*, do not worry. There is a state real estate license exam, but it is easy to study for and should not discourage you from pursuing a career as a real estate agent. In addition to the exam, some states require you to take between 30 and 90 hours of classroom or online instruction. Every state has a different licensing system, so be sure to contact your state's real estate licensing commission.

Even if your state does not require coursework, it is a good idea to take a few classes in real estate and finance. Having an understanding of concepts such as mortgage financing and property development will help you stand out among the competition. Those who cannot afford college-level courses or do not have time to pursue a degree can take courses at their local real estate association. In addition, some of the larger firms offer formal training for both beginners and experienced agents.

Finally, it is important to remember that personality is just as important as education in this field. Prospective employees are looking for friendly, self-motivated individuals who enjoy working with people, are good at sales, and have a passion for real estate, be it architecture, interiors, or property development.

You Are Here

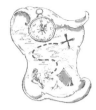

To see if you have what it takes to become a real estate agent, ask yourself these questions.

Do you have any sales experience? You might enjoy looking at real estate, but unless you have the sales skills to back it up, you will not get very far in this industry. Agents spend most of their time selling themselves to potential clients or emphasizing a property's selling points to potential buyers. Previous sales experience—even if it was just a part-time job at a retail chain—can help you determine whether or not you have an appetite for sales. Are you confident? Do you enjoy conversing with different types of people? Can you see both sides of an argument? These skills are often essential to sales.

Are you good with people? One of the keys to long-term success as an agent is developing strong client relations. Little things like having a good memory for names or being able to recall particulars from a previous conversation can really make a difference. More importantly, agents need to be able to work around their client's schedule, even if that means coming into the office at night or meeting with clients over the weekend.

Can you manage your own schedule? Most agents work on commission, which means that they have to be very self-motivated in order to achieve financial success. Those who have difficulty managing their own schedule and prefer the security of a steady paycheck might want to think twice before committing themselves to this profession. Real estate is a great opportunity for those who are very self-motivated, detail-oriented, and hate being stuck behind a desk.

Navigating the Terrain

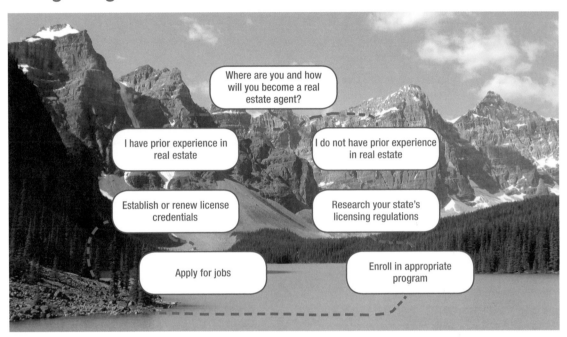

Where are you and how will you become a real estate agent?

I have prior experience in real estate

I do not have prior experience in real estate

Establish or renew license credentials

Research your state's licensing regulations

Apply for jobs

Enroll in appropriate program

Organizing Your Expedition

Be fully prepared to start the journey.

Decide on a destination. One of the luxuries of being a real estate agent is that you can work anywhere. Every community needs a real estate agent, so if you are really interested in becoming one, you should start thinking about where you would like to live and what sort of properties you would like to sell. The competition in real estate can be cutthroat, so it is often a good idea to start out in a community where you have a built-in network of friends and family.

Scout the terrain. Take a break from your license exam studying and go to a few open houses. Not only will it give you a good sense of how much real estate goes for in your area, you will also get to see an agent in action. Open houses are a good way to talk to agents and see how they interact with potential buyers. In addition, you might want to consider working as an assistant at a local real estate firm. Working for a firm or self-employed broker is a great way to become familiar with an agent's routine and make valuable connections along the way. With related work experience under your belt, you are almost guaranteed a position at an established agency.

Find the path that's right for you. Once you have decided where you would like to work, it is time to start marketing yourself. Agents generate a lot of business through word of mouth, so do not be afraid to promote yourself. Tell friends, colleagues, schoolteachers, aunts, cousins, and anyone else who will listen that you are getting into real estate. Business cards and mailers are also effective tools for self-promotion. The key is to get your name out in the community.

Landmarks

If you are in your twenties . . . This is the perfect time to take classes in real estate or possibly even obtain a degree. The competition from established agents can be tough, so try to find a mentor who will guide you through the practical aspects of the job, including the use of computers to locate or list available properties and identify sources of financing. If you stand out early on, you are guaranteed success in the coming years.

If you are in your thirties or forties . . . If you are looking to start a new career or make some extra cash for the family, start studying for the real estate license exam. Most buyers are in their thirties or forties, so you probably have a lot of friends who are looking for homes. Use this built-in network to your advantage. And do not forget, there are a lot of part-time jobs available in real estate, so you do not have to miss out on family time.

If you are in your fifties . . . This is a great time to get involved in real estate. As you know, the training is minimal so you can

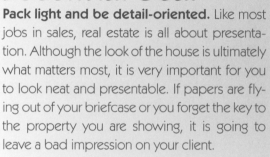

Essential Gear

Pack light and be detail-oriented. Like most jobs in sales, real estate is all about presentation. Although the look of the house is ultimately what matters most, it is very important for you to look neat and presentable. If papers are flying out of your briefcase or you forget the key to the property you are showing, it is going to leave a bad impression on your client.

Notes from the Field

Lamonta Pierson
Realtor, Hollywoodland Realty Co.
Los Angeles, California

What were you doing before you got into real estate?

I graduated from the Cincinnati Conservatory of Music and began working as a model and singer. At the age of 30, I decided that it was time for a change. You cannot go on modeling and singing forever, and I also had a family to support.

Why did you decide to pursue a career in real estate?

My husband, who worked in show business at the time, had stopped working, so I started looking into different types of employment. I wanted an interesting and lively job, but at the same time, I needed to have flexible hours so that I could spend time with my family and continue painting. A friend of mine mentioned real estate, and I liked the idea of matching people up with properties. I also liked the idea of owning a nice home, so I thought I would give real estate a try. Many years later, I am still working as an agent, I am still painting, and I now own a historical house that is within walking distance of my office.

What was involved in terms of education/training and getting your first job?

I took some continuing education classes to prepare for the California real estate licensing exam. Once you become an agent, every few years you are required by law to take an extension course that covers ethics, forms, and so on. After I passed the exam, I was hired at an established agency in Burbank.

get started in less than a year. It is a plus if you are a homeowner, because you can relate to what clients are going through as they prepare to make their purchases. If you have any background in real estate, marketing, construction, sales, or interior design, you should be able to secure a well-paying job without much training.

If you are over sixty . . . You have witnessed a lot of swings in the real estate market and probably have a better idea of property values than most agents starting out. Use your knowledge and wisdom to your advantage when applying for jobs, and remember that many real estate agencies offer part-time work.

Further Resources

The **National Association of Realtors** has been servicing members for over a century. It is a great site for networking, finding online real estate courses, and reading up on industry trends.   http://www.realtor.org

Internet Crusade is one of the most well respected online real estate communities. You can chat with agents, start your own Realblog, or join forums.   http://www.internetcrusade.com

Trulia is a great site for those interested in learning about a particular region's real estate market.   http://www.trulia.com

Property Manager

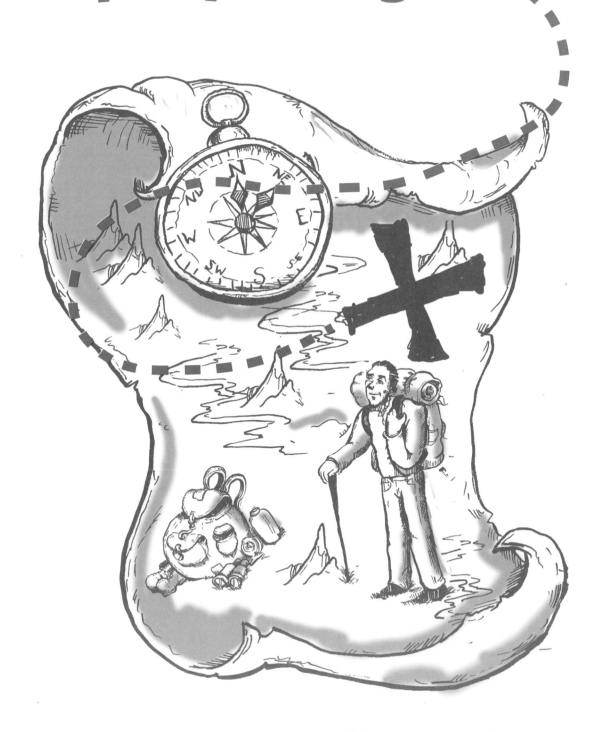

Property Manager

Career Compasses

Get your bearings on what it takes to become a property manager.

Communication Skills to help you handle different personalities and delicate situations (40%)

Ability to Manage Stress to meet the demands of tenants who rely on you to keep the property clean and safe (30%)

Mathematical Skills for handling financial operations and making sure that the property generates revenue (20%)

Organizational Skills to ensure all tasks are completed in a timely and orderly fashion (10%)

Destination: Property Manager

Commercial real estate is a multi-trillion dollar industry that fuels our economy and shapes our communities. Retail stores, office spaces, shopping centers, and industrial buildings all fall under the commercial real estate umbrella, and it is the property manager's job to ensure that these properties generate revenue.

11

Commercial property managers handle the maintenance, security, and financial operations for properties ranging from mom-and-pop restaurants to corporate office buildings. The day-to-day duties of the job vary depending on where you work and how much experience you have. Managers who work desk jobs at property management firms typically oversee the maintenance and revenue of a number of properties, whereas onsite property managers are in charge of overseeing a single property.

Essential Gear

Do not put all your eggs in one basket. If you only manage one property and the company goes out of business or suddenly vacates the building, it can leave you financially devastated. Those just starting out are better off managing a multi-tenant building, so that they can spread the risk over different organizations and companies.

Those just starting out often begin as onsite managers because the job involves more hands-on experience. As an onsite manager, you spend a great deal of time responding to tenant complaints, purchasing supplies, and monitoring the grounds to determine if any repairs are needed. In addition to maintenance and security, you are also in charge of advertising vacancies. Whenever a tenant moves out, onsite managers advertise the property, show it to prospective tenants, and make sure that any agreed upon improvements—such as new carpeting, lighting, or security cameras—are put into place before the new tenant moves in. On top of all this, onsite managers also collect the rent, keep up-to-date records of expenditures and submit expense reports to property owners.

Approximately half of the onsite commercial property managers in the United States work for property management firms. The rest are self-employed. Those who opt to work for themselves are typically hired on a contract basis by landlords. After working as an onsite manager for several years, many opt to take a desk job at a property management firm. Office managers typically handle contracts, negotiations, and legal issues. For example, if a janitorial company's contract expires, it is the office manager who evaluates their performance and makes the decision to renew the contract, renegotiate it, or put in a bid with another company. Although the job requires a lot of paperwork and telephone calls, office managers still spend a fair amount of time away from the desk. They work closely with onsite managers and frequently visit their assigned properties, particularly when contractors are working on major repairs or renovations.

Regardless of whether you work onsite, in an office, or for yourself, being a commercial property manager involves hard work, dedication, and around the clock assistance. As a commercial property manager, you are the primary liaison between the tenant and the landlord, which means that you must exercise patience and diplomacy on a regular basis. One property manager joked that the job is a constant game of good cop/bad cop. One day you are settling a dispute over parking spots and the next day you are banging on a tenant's door for the rent. It is hard work, but if you are good in a crisis situation and are interested in real estate management, this may be the job for you.

Although there are no major requirements to become a property manager, most major firms ask that you have a bachelor's or associate's degree. Even if you plan on striking out on your own, it is a good idea to enroll in a two- or four-year degree program in business administration, accounting, or real estate. If you cannot afford a degree, professional organizations such as the Institute of Real Estate Management (IREM) offer short-term training programs. These courses can teach you the basics of business management as well as expand your knowledge of specialized subjects such as the operation and maintenance of building mechanical systems, the enhancement of property values, business and real estate law, tenant relations, accounting, and reserve funding. In addition, IREM also offers a certification exam, which property managers in subsidized federal housing and other areas of the public sector must pass before entering the field. The exam is not required for those in the commercial sector, but more and more commercial property managers are becoming certified because it establishes credibility and sets them apart from the competition.

Essential Gear

Go Green! Commercial property managers who promote sustainable living are very much in demand these days, and with good reason. Eco-friendly properties are not only good for the environment, they also save money on energy bills, increase the value of the property, and attract better quality tenants. There are many small things that managers are doing to reduce a building's carbon imprint, such as using florescent bulbs instead of incandescent ones or separating waste at the point of source. If you can come up with better ways to create sustainable commercial properties, you will be in business for a long time.

You Are Here

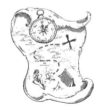

See if you have what it takes to manage a strip mall, storage facility, or office building.

Are you quick with numbers and good with people? A good property manager is adept at handling a variety of different personalities and can deal with potentially inflammatory situations in a tactful manner. Nobody wants to tell a mom-and-pop restaurant owner that they are going to be evicted unless they pay their rent, but part of your job as a property manager is to ensure that your property is generating revenue. This means collecting the rent on time, keeping maintenance bills low, and making sure that tenant disputes are resolved in a peaceful and timely manner. Enforcing the terms of the lease or rental agreement can be quite stressful, which is why aspirants should have strong communication skills and a flair for numbers.

Do you have any experience in building maintenance? You need to understand how buildings operate before you can manage one. Onsite managers, in particular, spend a large portion of their workday visiting building engineers, checking on the janitorial and maintenance staff, talking to contractors, and investigating leaks, break-ins, and electrical problems. Those who have prior experience in building maintenance and repair will find it much easier to handle the day-to-day problems of the job. Property managers are not expected to know everything about building maintenance, as it is a vast field that includes pipefitting, boiler making, welding, carpentry, and electrical repair. However, those interested in becoming a commercial property manager should be able to speak the language of electricians, plumbers, and other maintenance staff.

Are you proactive and able to multi-task? The best property managers are quick-minded and proactive. If you can anticipate a potential problem, such as a faulty elevator cable or dim lighting in a stairwell, it can save money—and, in some cases, prevent injuries and lawsuits. When things do fall apart, a manager must act quickly and decisively. It is also important to stay on top of all your other responsibilities. Mundane tasks, such as coordinating garbage removal, cannot fall to the wayside just because a tenant unexpectedly moves out or a burglary occurs. Those who succeed in this business are usually adept at multi-tasking.

Organizing Your Expedition

Prepare yourself for a career in property management.

Decide on a destination. As you can see, many paths lead to commercial property management. If you can identify an area of expertise and gain some experience in that field, you will certainly standout from the competition. Some aspiring managers chose to work at a real estate agency because it teaches you how to market and show properties; others go into maintenance and repair because expertise in building mechanical systems is highly sought after in property management. If you are interested in working at an office, managerial experience is an invaluable way to get your foot in the door. Property management firms look for people who have managed retail stores, offices, warehouses, and so on.

Navigating the Terrain

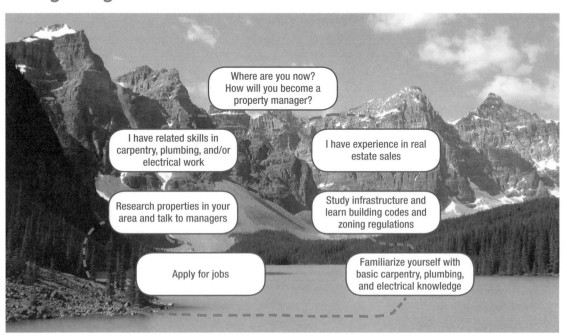

Where are you now? How will you become a property manager?

I have related skills in carpentry, plumbing, and/or electrical work

I have experience in real estate sales

Research properties in your area and talk to managers

Study infrastructure and learn building codes and zoning regulations

Apply for jobs

Familiarize yourself with basic carpentry, plumbing, and electrical knowledge

Notes from the Field
Susan Shepard
Property manager, Maguire Building Properties
Los Angeles, California

Why did you decide to pursue a career in commercial property management?
I was working in sales for many years and one day I decided to leave the field. I took a job working for a construction manager on a project in downtown San Antonio, Texas. When the building was completed, he asked me if I would be interested in the property management field. I did not really know what it was all about, but it sounded like a new challenge. At the time, I was not too heavily invested in it, but I thought I would give it a try and if it did not work out I would try something else. Nineteen years later, I am still doing it.

How did you make the transition?
There was not too much of a transition. I knew a great deal about the building from having been around during construction, so I basically moved from an administrative assistant role to an assistant property management position.

What was involved in terms of education/training?
Most of my training was on the job. I had a great supervisor who had been in the business for a number of years. Although he was in Houston

Scout the terrain. Like most jobs in the real estate industry, commercial property management is susceptible to market changes. When a particular real market is down, leases will be broken and properties will be foreclosed. All this can negatively affect a commercial property manager, so the best way to protect yourself from market insecurities is to do your homework. Before you start to manage a property, research the surrounding area. Are there a lot of vacancies? If so, you might want to consider looking at properties in a more bustling district. You should also keep up with the local news. For example, if you are thinking about managing a local coffee shop, you should know if a Starbucks is about to open in the area.

Find the path that's right for you. Although many of the skills necessary to becoming a commercial property manager are learned on the

and I was in San Antonio, he visited frequently and I ran a lot of my decisions through him. His mentorship was invaluable to me. Once I was "in the business" I started taking classes through Building Owner's and Manager's Association (BOMA) and received my Real Property Administrators (RPA) certification through them. After that, I took courses through the Institute of Real Estate Management (IREM) to get my Certified Property Manager (CPM) designation. Both are highly recognized designations in the business and I was fortunate enough to work for a company that paid for my classes. The rest of my education has been common sense and on-the-job training. It is not really possible to "train" someone for this job because there are so many variables and people involved. You see something new every day in this business because it is mostly about your tenants, all of whom are unique.

What are the keys to success as a commercial property manager?

Just as "location, location, location" is the key to the real estate business, "common sense, common sense, common sense" is the key to this business. You have to see things in shades of grey most of the time because you are dealing with a bunch of different personalities. Patience helps, as does being flexible. Property management is like running a very large household. You have to know how to maintain order, keep everything clean and secure, pay the bills, budget yourself, and watch over your "kids" (i.e. the tenants).

job, nowadays most employers want to see coursework or a degree on your résumé. Luckily, commercial property management involves a variety of skill sets, meaning that you have a lot of different options in the way of studying. There are property management courses, but you do not need to limit yourself to just real estate classes. Many successful property managers have degrees in business, accounting, communications, engineering, and even sociology.

Landmarks

If you are in your twenties . . . This is the perfect time to study property management and widen your area of expertise. Enroll in a course at a local college or take a job in a related field. Many young people find work as assistants at property management firms. This is one of the best ways to learn about the industry and decide if it is the right fit for you.

If you are in your thirties or forties . . . You still have the drive and determination to tackle a new industry and make a name for yourself. If you have ever worked in sales, marketing, building maintenance, or management, it is relatively easy to make the transition into commercial property management. As a newcomer, you are usually put in charge of one property, but after four or five years you will be given a large complex of buildings to manage. This means that your salary will increase as well your responsibilities.

If you are in your fifties . . . You probably have a lot of work experience, and unlike most of the competition, you have a lot of life experience to draw from as well. Finding employment at a property management firm should be easy, particularly if you have ever worked in real estate or management.

If you are over sixty . . . Most onsite manager positions are given to young people with less work experience, but firms are always looking for experienced and reliable office managers who can command authority and respect. When speaking with potential employers, emphasize skilled trades such as plumbing or electrical work that you may have on your résumé.

Further Resources

The **Building Owners and Managers Association** is an international association that provides excellent information on office building development, leasing, building operating costs, local and national building codes, and legislation. http://www.boma.org

The **Institute of Real Estate Management** has been around for almost 75 years and is the only professional management association serving both the multi-family and commercial real estate sectors. http://www.irem.org

The *Journal of Property Management* is a trade publication with excellent articles on industry trends and developments. You can find recent issues of the publication online or at certain library branches. http://www.irem.org/sechome.cfm?sec=JPM

Landlord

Landlord

Career Compasses

Get your bearings on what it takes to become a landlord.

Caring about the upkeep of your property and the safety of your tenants (40%)

Relevant Knowledge of your local real estate market (20%)

Communication Skills to make tenants feel at home and deal with any complaints or problems that they may bring to you (20%)

Ability to Manage Stress when a faucet breaks or a toilet overflows (20%)

Destination: Landlord

The textbook definition of a landlord is a landowner who leases properties, such as apartments, houses, or condominiums, to businesses or individuals, but the job involves so much more than just leasing properties and collecting rent. As a landlord, you deal with everything from leaky faucets and locksmiths to lawsuits and deaths on the property. Landlords spend a lot of time researching properties, obtaining financing, managing tenants, dealing with repairs, and making sure that all the bills are paid. It is a job that requires you to wear a lot of hats including, on occasion, a hard hat. When admiring a beautiful brownstone or a stately building, most people give credit to the architect, but if it were not for landlords, many of the houses and buildings we so admire would be falling down or flattened altogether.

Whether you are investing in a large warehouse or a small duplex, buying real estate requires time, money, and a certain amount of business savvy. Although there is never a shortage of attractive properties on the market, finding one that can cover your maintenance, repairs, insurance, taxes, and mortgage payments can be surprisingly difficult. A lot of people assume that once you have acquired a decent rental property you are set for life, but dealing with maintenance issues—not to mention deadbeat renters— requires a lot of hard work and responsibility. Landlords who own multiple properties or have a second job typically hire a property manager to handle maintenance and repairs, but in many instances, it is the landlord who manages the property and handles all the tenant complaints.

In addition to caring for the property, a landlord needs to care for the safety and wellbeing of the tenants. A lot of landlords cut corners by installing cheap smoke alarms or pre-owned water heaters. This may save money in the short term, but it could cost you dearly down the line. If a fire occurs inside of your properties, and it is discovered that you installed a cheap fire alarm or that the smoke detector's batteries were dead, your tenant could go after you in court.

Essential Gear

Get your name out there. Marketing and promoting yourself is very important, particularly if you invest in a suburban or rural setting. Those just starting out should contact the personnel at local colleges, medical offices, or corporations and let them know that you have rental properties available. If personnel departments are willing to refer one or two people to you, it could save you the time and trouble of running a vacancy ad in a local newspaper.

One of the major components of this job is screening tenants. Landlords who do not screen tenants invariably end up dealing with property damage, past-due rent, midnight move-outs, and noise violations. Landlords should always look into a potential tenant's credit and criminal history. It may seem drastic, but an irresponsible tenant can put you on the path to financial ruin.

As you can see, being a landlord involves more than just leasing properties and making sure that everyone's rent comes in on time. The job involves a lot of hard work, responsibility, and clogged toilets, but if you work hard and invest wisely, there is the potential for great financial gain.

Essential Gear

Insurance ensures success. There are all sorts of personal injury claims that can occur inside or outside your property, so landlords should make sure that their property is adequately insured for personal injury and liability. It is also important to have an attorney to help protect your investment in the event that there is property damage.

In addition, you will discover that there are great benefits to becoming a landlord, not the least of which being the flexible hours. Occasionally landlords receive a middle-of-the-night call that they have to respond to, but for the most part, they are able to create their own schedule. It is the perfect job for an independent person who wants to start a business or a creative type who wants to earn a stable income. Landlords who buy multi-tenant properties, such as duplexes or apartment buildings, can also live rent-free in one of their units. This is a good idea for those just starting out because it saves money and allows you to keep a close eye on your property.

For some people, the job's biggest allure is that there are no degree requirements. To become a landlord all you technically need is to own land. However, if you do not have any prior knowledge or experience in the field, you should take a course on real estate investing before buying a property. In addition, there are a number of local and state laws that landlords should research before renting their property. For example, in San Francisco landlords are required to provide heating capable of maintaining a room temperature of at least 68 degrees. If landlords do not adhere to this housing code, it could result in a fine from the city.

There are many more laws and codes that are specific to your area, so it is important for you to educate yourself. Most community colleges and local universities offer a variety of courses on real estate and property management. If you cannot afford to take a class, Web sites such as the Apartment Owners Association offer online seminars that will teach you the basics of landlord tenant laws and formal documents, such as the rental application and agreement. Understanding the rental agreement is particularly important because a poorly worded or outdated form can make evicting a problem tenant expensive, if not impossible.

You Are Here

Before hanging up a vacancy sign, see if you have the necessary skills to become a landlord.

Are you a self-starter with do-it-yourself skills? In order to succeed as a landlord, you must have an entrepreneurial spirit and a unique brand of business savvy. Investing in real estate requires a different set of skills than investing in stocks or bonds. When you are playing the stock market, you put a stock in a brokerage account and simply wait for it to increase in value. With real estate you have to put hard work and actual labor into your investment. We have all heard the expression, "things do not just fix themselves," but for landlords this takes on greater meaning. Some landlords hire property managers to take care of maintenance and repair issues, but managers can eat up 10 percent of your rental income. If you are handy with a hammer, wrench, or trowel, you will save a lot of money in this profession.

Do you have any experience in the real estate industry? Although previous real estate experience is not a prerequisite, working at a real estate agency or property management company is a great way to prepare for the responsibilities of being a landlord. It will also give you a good sense of your local real estate market and help you determine whether you have the proper finances to invest in real estate. Landlords ideally want a property that will give them a minimum amount of stress and a maximum amount of profit, but finding such a property involves a lot of research and a certain amount of financial risk. Before becoming a landlord, you need to be sure that you are committed to buying and maintaining a property.

Are you a patient and open-minded individual? One of the best parts about being a landlord is that you get to meet a variety of different people. However, there are occasions when being a landlord is like having a roommate. You have to put up with habits that may not correspond to yours—and occasionally you have issues with property damage. It is a job that requires patience, tolerance, and an open mind. The Fair Housing Law of 1968 states that "everyone, regardless of sex, race, color, religion, ancestry or national origin are entitled to full and equal ac-

Navigating the Terrain

What is your best path to becoming a landlord?

Invest in an affordable property such as a duplex

Consider remodeling or updating as necessary

Become familiar with tenant laws and tax policies

Acquire renters and look to reinvest in the property

commodations." Nowadays, states adamantly enforce this law, so landlords with any sort of prejudice are liable to face serious discrimination lawsuits.

Organizing Your Expedition

It is time to dust off your toolbox and get to work as a landlord.

Decide on a destination. One of the perks of being a landlord is that you can work virtually anywhere. Thus, the big decision is not where to live, but what to buy. The first property that a new landlord buys is typically a duplex because it allows the landlord to live in one unit and rent out the other. Duplexes are the most affordable investments, however, they are not the most lucrative. If you have saved enough money, you might want to consider buying an apartment complex. If you buy a complex in an up-and-coming area or find a crumbling complex and do a nice job remodeling the units, you have the potential to make a lot of money.

Scout the terrain. Before becoming a landlord it is a good idea to learn the basics of carpentry, plumbing, electrical wiring, and basic home maintenance. You might want to try renovating something basic such as a garage. Even the handiest of landlords has to call a repair person every now and then, but if you know how much a water heater costs or how long it takes to fix a leak in the ceiling, you are less likely to get ripped off.

Find the path that's right for you. It used to be that investing in real estate yielded steady returns, but thanks to a faltering economy and the recent crisis in subprime home mortgage debt, real estate has become a very volatile industry. Although employment opportunities for landlords are growing, it has become very difficult for landlords to make any returns on their investment. If you are serious about making a living as a landlord, you need to be financially prepared for economic downturns and have money saved away in the event that your mortgage rates rise or you have to lower your rent.

Landmarks

If you are in your twenties . . . Now is the perfect time to enroll in a two- or four-year college to study real estate, business, or property management. It may cost you money now, but getting an education in real estate will make you more money down the line.

If you are in your thirties or forties . . . You may have already saved up enough money to invest in a property. Perhaps you have a job and are simply looking to supplement the family income by buying a property and renting it out. You can keep a steady job and be a landlord, though if you start to accumulate a lot of properties you might have to leave your job or hire a property manager.

If you are in your fifties . . . You probably own a home already and have a good understanding of your local real estate market. You might also have a lot of money saved up, which means that you can invest in larger properties that have a greater potential for return. Before investing in any properties, you should take an extension course or online seminar to educate yourself on tax incentives and landlord tenant laws.

Notes from the Field

Patricia Carroll
Landlord
Los Angeles, California

What were you doing before you started working as a landlord?

I have been "in" real estate since as long as I can remember. My parents worked in real estate, so it was something I grew up with. However, I did not actually get involved in the business until I was in my forties. Before that, I lived in Paris where I had an art and graphic design magazine distribution business. I also worked in advertising for Condé Nast. These experiences helped me think broadly, which is important if you want to become a landlord.

Why did you decide to pursue a career in real estate?

I was surrounded by real estate investing as a child, so it was always in the back of my mind. I decided to pursue a career as a landlord because it seemed much more fun than investing in the stock market

If you are over sixty . . . If you are getting ready to retire but want to remain active, being a landlord is the perfect profession. Landlords make their own schedule and the job is full of surprises, so you never get bored. Before investing in any real estate, you should find a reliable property management company that can handle all of the physical requirements that come with the job.

Further Resources

The **American Apartment Owners Association** is a membership organization that offers excellent online seminars and free rental application forms. It also gives you links to property management companies and credit report bureaus.   http://www.american-apartment-owners-association.org

The Unofficial Guide to Real Estate Investing by Spencer Strauss and Martin Stone is a must-read book for those wishing to know more about the role of a landlord. It can be hard to make real estate investing sound

and certainly easier to understand. I have always enjoyed meeting new people, so I wanted to invest in interesting properties that would attract interesting tenants. Another plus was that I could manage properties while pursing other aspects of my career. Once I figured out how to effectively manage my properties, I was able to do other things with my life, and I knew that I could always fall back on the steady profits I received from being a landlord.

What was involved in terms of education/training and landing your first job?
My first job was easy as it involved managing a property that my parents owned. From there, I started investing in my own properties. The real estate industry is never stagnant, so you have to grow to keep up with it. One of the things I love about working in real estate is that the education and training never stops. There are continuing education courses, specific training for designations, constant legal training, and community outreach. Above all else, you learn a tremendous amount just from interacting with tenants.

lively on paper, but these guys do a good job of explaining complicated topics, such as specialty loans, seller financing, and tax breaks, in an entertaining and reader-friendly manner.

Landlord Association.org bills itself as the most comprehensive Web site for landlords, and it appears to be just that. It provides you with landlord tenant laws for all 50 states, the latest industry news, and a glossary of real estate terms. There are also discussion forums and online networking opportunities.   http://www.landlordassociation.org

Real Estate Developer

Real Estate Developer

Career Compasses

Get your bearings on what it takes to become a real estate developer.

Communication Skills to effectively work with a variety of people, from construction workers and architects to brokers and land surveyors (30%)

Ability to Manage Stress when financing falls through or an investment stops generating a profit (30%)

Mathematical Skills to compute the costs of building or renovating a property and be able to calculate profit margins (20%)

Relevant Knowledge of the real estate market and finance world (20%)

Destination: Real Estate Developer

As the population grows, so does the role of the real estate developer whose job it is to build large-scale residential, industrial, and commercial properties. Developers use construction experience and community influence to build homes that benefit the local population and generate profit. It is a challenging job that requires entrepreneurial instincts and strong communication skills. Developers, particularly those who run their own company, often work long hours and weekends.

Much of this time is spent away from the office, scouting for new development projects, visiting construction sites, or meeting with bankers, architects, contractors, and so on. It is an active job, but if you enjoy meeting new people and want to participate in community development, this may be the field for you.

Once a tract of land has been selected, the first thing that the developer or development firm does is secure enough "seed" money to purchase the land. From this point forward, the development process varies depending on what is being built and who is building it. For example, a shopping mall is going to have different building requirements than a residential community. The day-to-day responsibilities of the job also vary depending on whether the developer specializes in finance, construction, or recruitment. Those involved in finance typically work with banks, government agencies, and financial consultants to analyze the cost, risk, and benefits of a project. They also help negotiate deals and are therefore at their busiest during pre-development. Construction liaisons usually come on board once ground has been broken. They are responsible for overseeing all aspects of construction. They must also ensure that safety regulations are being upheld and all local building codes are met. When construction is nearing completion, development recruiters are hired to oversee sales. They put together statistics and models to incite potential buyers or renters. Although their job does not require a background in construction, it is important for recruiters to have an understanding of the process for scheduling purposes. For example, if there are delays in a construction project—and there usually are—it is the recruiter who has to deal with angry tenants demanding to be compensated for their wait.

Essential Gear

Find a good accountant. The job of a developer can be very stressful and involves a lot of financial paperwork. Keeping your finances straight is very important in development, but most developers do not have time to juggle the books, which is why it is important to hire a good accountant. Not only do you want an accountant with a good track record, it is also important to find someone with whom you get along.

Development is not just about building new homes. It is also about building strong relations with contractors, architects, construction workers, and the like. Regardless of where you work, every developer is tasked with the responsibility of assembling a team of professionals to address the environmental, economic, physical, and political demands of development projects. Indeed, one of the most exciting parts of the job is working with a diverse group of experts and learning from them. For example, if a development company is building on or near an environmentally sensitive area such as wetlands or a protected forest, the company might need to hire an environmental consulting firm to advice on how to develop property without damaging natural habitats.

Essential Gear

Learn the ins and outs of the Multiple Listings Service (MLS). When a developer is ready to invest, the best way to conduct research on a potential property or tract of land is to use a Multiple Listings Service. Most MLS systems are restricted to real estate brokers and agents, but access is becoming more open as Internet sites offer the public the ability to view portions of MLS listings. Sometimes brokers will also give you access to their systems.

In addition to people skills, development requires forward thinking and creative financing, which is why many successful developers have backgrounds in business or finance. Technically speaking, there are no educational requirements to become a developer. However, most employers will not hire someone who does not have a bachelor's or associate's degree. Although lack of an undergraduate or graduate degree does not necessarily prevent a qualified candidate from a successful career, a degree does help get that first job interview or make the right connections. Some of the more useful degrees to pursue are business administration, marketing, finance, or real estate analysis. That said, programs in more artistic fields such as architecture or urban planning can give a potential developer an edge by exposing him or her to the actual development process, as opposed to just the business side of things. Such courses of study are highly recommended—and at some jobs even required—for employment. If you cannot afford to enroll in a program, another approach is to work at a broker leasing agency. Brokers are known for working directly with developers to seek potential buyers, so one would be able to see the development process firsthand from start to finish.

You Are Here

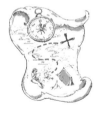

See if you have what it takes to develop a career in this field.

Are you willing to take financial risks? Development requires a large amount of money up front and there is never a guarantee of return. It is one of the riskiest jobs in real estate, but with that risk comes the opportunity for great financial reward. Some developers own their own firms and earn $1 million or more a year, while others experience streaks of unsuccessful investments.

Even at the corporate level, a real estate developer's earnings often depend on unpredictable factors, such as geographic trends and the condition of the economy. If you are someone who thrives on routine and needs a steady income, this may not be the job for you. Conversely, if you have an entrepreneurial spirit and strong money management skills, you will go far as a developer.

Are you a creative problem solver with a good eye for real estate? Most developers will tell you that the biggest house with the best view is not necessarily the best investment. Often times, it is those decrepit or abandoned buildings—sometimes referred to as "white elephants" in the development industry—that have the best profit potential. To be a successful developer, you need to have a creative vision and be one step ahead of real estate trends. Let's say there is an old mill at the edge of an up-and-coming town. A good developer will immediately see the property's unrealized potential and come up with a creative plan that best utilizes the space and addresses any rehabilitation challenges.

Are you a team player? If you are serious about development, you should enjoy working with a variety of different people. As much of what a developer does on a day-to-day basis is meet with people and oversee construction.

Developers work with everyone from architects and financiers to building inspectors and contractors. Large development companies often have in-house construction and finance teams, but if you work at a small development company with only one principal, the task of hiring architects, lawyers, building inspectors, and construction companies can be considerable.

Navigating the Terrain

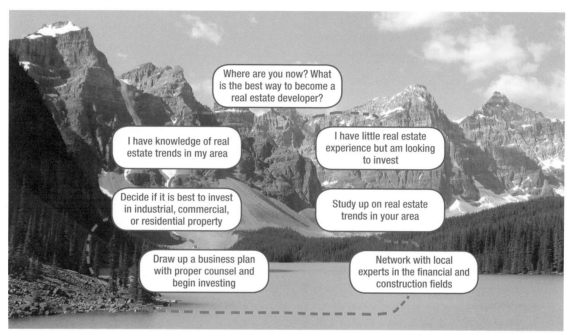

Where are you now? What is the best way to become a real estate developer?

I have knowledge of real estate trends in my area

I have little real estate experience but am looking to invest

Decide if it is best to invest in industrial, commercial, or residential property

Study up on real estate trends in your area

Draw up a business plan with proper counsel and begin investing

Network with local experts in the financial and construction fields

Organizing Your Expedition

Construct a career for yourself as a real estate developer.

Decide on a destination. Poor cash flow is the primary cause of business failure for real estate developers. Those who want to start their own business should know how to draw up a winning business plan, assemble a team of experts, install basic cost control systems, and set up accounting and bookkeeping procedures. Although there are many self-employed developers, an equal number work for large companies. It is important to decide what type of office environment suits you best. It is also important to ascertain what sort of development you want to specialize in—industrial, commercial, or residential.

Scout the terrain. Real estate development is all about resourcefulness and finding the right property at the right time. For example, Donald Trump built his real estate fortune by investing in Manhattan real estate at a time

Notes from the Field

Erica Cashman Shevlin
Real estate developer, Jay M. Cashman, Inc.
Quincy, Massachusetts

What were you doing before you became involved in real estate development?

I was a singer/songwriter living in New York City before I changed careers. I produced three records and toured the northeast with my band.

Why did you decide to pursue a career in development?

When I turned 26 I decided that I could not spend the rest of my life on the road touring. I was a little lost as to what to do next, so my father pushed me into working for him in real estate. He has a mid-sized real estate development company that spun out of his construction company.

What was involved in terms of education and training?

I had little formal training. I took a few courses at NYU, but mostly I just worked hard and asked a lot of questions. I was working with all men and most of them had been in real estate their entire lives. Being

when the city was in a financial slump and tremendous tax cuts were being offered to investors. He also took over troubled construction projects that had gone over budget and was able to charge only his costs. This sort of knowledge and creative thinking is necessary in order to succeed in the real estate industry. If you are thinking of investing in a place yourself, do your research and do not judge a property by its looks. Often times, it is better to have the worst property on the best block. Remember, you can always change the look of a place, but you can never change its location.

Find the path that's right for you. Most aspiring developers who want to work at the corporate level start out as assistants to senior developers. The job requires you to do a number of administrative duties, such as preparing reports, double-checking facts and figures, keeping track of files, and coordinating meetings. The hours are long and the work can be

the boss's daughter, no one cut me any slack. Real estate development is a sink or swim industry, so you really have to work hard.

What are the keys to success as a real estate developer?

Do not rely on brokers to do your homework and always verify what they tell you. There are a series of things I do when I am looking at buying a building or developing land. First off, I find out what the previous owners paid for the property and how much debt they have on it. You can find this information on multiple listings or at the assessor's office. If a property is overpriced or if the current owners paid more then it is worth, I usually stop there. If they paid fair money for the property, I then start on market research. For instance, I always check the absorption rate. I also want to understand where the market is going. Is price per square foot going up? Did more homes sell last year then the year before? How many homes are on the market in my price range now? What's the average day on the market? I then research who my competition would be. I also look at wetland maps and town regulations. My last piece of advice is to always expect the unexpected. There are many things that can get in the way of development, but if you do your homework right, you should be able to handle the bumps along the way.

tedious, but if you prove yourself worthy of the job, you are likely to be promoted to an associate position. Those who cannot find assistant positions or are interested in being a construction liaison at a development company might want to consider working in the construction industry for a few years. An understanding of basic engineering and construction principles will make you stand out amongst the competition. Also, those not familiar with the basic principles of finance might want to consider enrolling in a business or finance program.

Landmarks

If you are in your twenties . . . Because there is so much risk involved in development, it is important to learn as much as possible before diving into the field. Enroll in a business, finance, or real estate degree program, and take a full- or part-time job in any area of real estate. Now is also the time to get your personal finances in order, particularly if you plan on starting your own development company.

If you are in your thirties or forties . . . If you are an associate at a company, you should be trying to start your own projects. In order to do so, you need to network and establish contacts in finance, construction, and property management. If you are investing on your own, keep your personal expenses low. Once you start generating a profit, reinvest to increase your holdings.

If you are in your fifties . . . Find your area of expertise. Many development companies look for people who can head up their construction, finance, or sales divisions, so you might want to consider specializing in one of these three areas. If you run your own development company, you should be diversifying your portfolio and acquiring more prestigious properties where demand and price per square foot run high.

If you are over sixty . . . You have probably worked on multiple projects and are ready to start receiving a cut from your deals. Sometimes companies will offer you a percentage of a deal in exchange for a low base pay. The trade-off is usually worth it.

Further Resources

The **Urban Land Institute** is a nonprofit organization that offers a thriving online community dedicated to the open exchange of ideas and experience among local, national, and international industry leaders and policy makers. They are also known for their publications and online certification programs.   http://www.uli.org

NAIOP is a membership-based organization that provides networking opportunities for those interested in commercial, industrial, and mixed-use real estate development. They also offer a wide array of online seminars.   http://www.naiop.org

Builder

Builder

Career Compasses

Get your bearings on what it takes to become a builder.

Relevant Knowledge of carpentry, plumbing, bricklaying, and other construction trades as well as marketing, sales, supply chain management, and customer service (50%)

Organizational Skills to coordinate schedules, stay within budget, and make sure that construction is running smoothly (20%)

Communication Skills to liaise with homebuyers, contractors, construction workers, developers, and architects throughout the building process (20%)

Mathematical Skills to create estimates and work within budget (10%)

Destination: Builder

The residential home building market has come along way over the years, and it is largely thanks to the pioneering work of home builders whose job it is to build innovative homes at affordable prices. Builders oversee all aspects of construction, from the first shovel until the last nail. Most builders are skilled in several construction trades, including bricklaying, carpentry, and plastering. They also need to be able to read floor maps and inspect the quality of work being done by contractors and trade workers.

Although the job may be more physically demanding than most, there is a lot more to building than just sandblasters and hard hats. Builders obtain building permits, make sure the construction site is properly insured, establish work and payment schedules for their workers, write up warranties for the homeowners, and enforce safety regulations on the site. They are also in charge of bringing in the project on time and within budget. It is a tough job that requires a lot of responsibility, but most builders would agree that there is nothing like hoisting a shovel in the air and breaking ground on your first home.

The majority of custom builders are either self-employed or work for a national home building firm, such as Toll Brothers. The industry is further divided into two different types of builders: production home builders and custom home builders. Production builders construct model homes, condos, and suburban subdivisions on land that is owned by large building firms. Unlike custom builders who literally build one-of-a-kind homes, production builders typically work from only a handful of housing models, thereby enabling them to builder homes faster and for less money. A good production builder has constructed the same few models so many times that they have it refined to a science. There is little waste in terms of materials, which in turn, drives costs down and leads to even greater profits. Although production builders do not work with architects or designers, they usually offer customized options for model homes, floor layouts, and certain product features. Custom builders, on the other

Essential Gear

Be able to decipher aerial and floor maps.
Learning how to read and draw floor maps is integral to becoming a builder. If you are interested in going into production building or want to start your own company, it is important to consult an aerial map of your area before buying any land. Aerial maps, which are available for purchase online, have all available plots of land outlined in yellow.

hand, build custom home designs from scratch. Typically, they work with an architect who sketches a design that meets the homebuyer's needs. From there, the custom builder reviews it and gives an estimate of how much it will cost to build the house and how long it will take. Regardless of what line of building you are in, being a builder is an active job that involves long hours and tight deadlines. You also spend a fair amount of time traveling from your office base to construction sites.

Building is a broad field that involves many different skills. Although a high school diploma is the only official educational requirement, most employers look for builders who are certified in at least one construction trade and have some form of educational training. If you are serious about becoming a builder, there are plenty of vocational high schools and technical colleges that offer valuable experience in the construction trades. These schools teach you the basic principles of carpentry, plumbing, and electrical wiring as well as offering instruction on how to draw a floor plan, build

Essential Gear

Stock your toolbox. If you are serious about becoming a builder, there is no better way to show it than by having the right tools, machines, equipment, and materials of the trade. Although builders do not always use their personal tools for business, it is nevertheless important to stay on top of the latest designs and have fully functioning nailers, drills, sanders, wet dry vacuums, and so on.

a scale model, and develop a realty specification sheet. In addition to technical schools, many local home builder associations (HBAs) have industry/education partnership programs for aspiring builders and construction workers.

If you cannot afford college or have received a degree in another field, there are a number of different ways to obtain the necessary training, the most common of which are construction jobs. Another way to gain experience is through construction apprenticeship programs, which combine paid on-the-job training with classroom instruction. For example, a carpenter's apprentice will have the opportunity to meet with builders in the area and become familiar with common carpentry jobs, such as layout, form building, rough framing, and outside and inside finishing. In the classroom, carpentry apprentices learn safety, first aid, blueprint reading, and freehand sketching. Apprenticeships such as this are a great entry into the building profession. Once you have had construction experience, educational training, or a combination of the two, you should be prepared to take at least one certification exam. The licensure and certification requirements differ from state to state, so be sure to find out what your state requires.

You Are Here

Discover the building blocks to becoming a better builder.

Do you have experience in the construction trades? You cannot expect to build a structurally sound house without understanding the principles of carpentry, plumbing, site supervision, and other construction trades. Construction is one of the nation's largest industries with 8.3 million workers, so finding a job should be relatively easy. If you work hard and have the right amount of ambition, a construction job can sometimes act as a substitute for a college degree in that it opens doors to a plethora of interrelated trades and occupations.

Are you interested in architecture and building design? In order to really appreciate the job of a builder, you need to have a fundamental appreciation for architecture and design. Do you enjoy looking at certain types of architecture? Have you always wondered how things were built? If so, then a career in home building could be the perfect fit for you. On the surface, building homes is all about planning and paperwork, but when you get down to it, there is a lot of artistry in building, particularly in custom building. A successful builder has the eye of an architect and the pragmatism of an engineer. If you are already familiar with classical architecture and can explain the difference between an ionic and Doric column, you are on the right track. Those who are not familiar should consider taking a course before jumping head first into the building industry.

Are you a team player? This job requires you to be kind, respectful, and good with people. There is not a lot of repeat business in the building profession, so builders are always on the lookout for new clients. If you are good with sales and enjoy networking, you should not have a problem finding clients; however, it takes more than salesmanship to maintain a thriving home building company. Builders need to develop strong relationships with subcontractors, building product suppliers, and trade workers. A lot of builders overwork their trade workers and bargain down their rates, both of which can lead to a bad reputation and a decrease in productivity and profit. If you value your workers, not only will they respect you more, they will also work harder.

Navigating the Terrain

How will you become a builder?

Gain experience with a construction crew

Get certified in one or more specific areas, such as plumbing or electrical work

Talk to other subcontractors and make contacts in the field

Apply for jobs with building companies or start your own business

Organizing Your Expedition

Come up with a blueprint for success and stick to it.

Decide on a destination. When the real estate market is down, home building firms oftentimes reduce their workforce. If you are skilled in several construction trades and can build an assortment of housing models, you will always be a valuable asset to a company. For example, green construction is in high demand right now, so builders who know a lot about energy conversation, retrofitting, and electronically operated "smart" buildings are making a lot of money right now. Other specialties to consider are renovations, roof extensions, multi-family home construction, and technology transfer programs. If you are thinking of starting your own company, it is critical to have more than one area of specialization—that way you can expand and diversify your business model.

Scout the terrain. It is important to keep up-to-date on new construction products, materials, and practices. Housingzone.com and Toolbase. org are great sites to explore, but the best way to stay ahead of the curve is to be active in the construction community. Join a trade association, visit a few trade shows, and talk to subcontractors and manufacturers. Not only will you make important contacts, you will also learn a lot about the industry.

Find the path that's right for you. Before applying for jobs as a home builder, most builders join a construction crew or work as an apprentice to a carpenter, plumber, or electrician. After a few years on the job, construction workers typically graduate to crew leader and apprentices complete their programs and are sometimes offered positions within the company. Regardless of what path you take, it is a good idea to get certified in a field of interest before looking for building jobs or starting your own business. There are dozens of certifications available in the construction trades. Additionally, associations such as the National Association of Home Builders offer certification programs in a variety of specialized areas, including renovation, green construction and residential construction superintendent designations.

Landmarks

If you are in your twenties . . . This is the best time to gain educational and on-the-job experience in construction. These are your critical decision-making years, so now is the time to decide whether you would like to become a custom or production builder.

If you are in your thirties or forties . . . If you already have some construction or contracting experience, you should be able to find work as a custom or production builder. If you have not already done so, join a few associations and start making contacts in the field. Networking is particularly important if you plan on starting your own business.

If you are in your fifties . . . You probably have access to capital and are capable of building several different home models, so if you are inclined to start your own business, this is a good time to do it. Hire a lead

Notes from the Field
Mark Dorsey
Builder, Mark M. Dorsey, Inc.
Freeport, Maine

What were you doing before you became involved in building?

I graduated from Bowdoin College in 1978. At the time, there was still a bit of a hangover from the hippie era, and it was fashionable to drop out of the usual corporate track and do your own thing. Since I was passionate about architecture and had no interest in corporate life anyway, I decided to get into building.

Why did you decide to pursue a career in building?

Architecture, particularly New England architecture, was always an interest of mine. As soon as I got my driver's license, I started driving around the coast of Maine poking into all the little coastal areas that had escaped modern blight. When I first got into building, I was an arrogant youth who thought it was my mission to stamp out the ugly architecture of expedience, which was the norm in those days.

How did you make the transition?

Before starting my own business, I spent six years working for a local builder who built what passed for high-end homes. I also took the Shelter Institute course thinking it would give me a good overview of the construction industry. In the end, however, my on-the-job training proved much more useful.

What are the keys to success as a builder?

If I really knew the answer to this question, I would probably be relaxing on a private island in the Bahamas. Having said that, I think a love of architecture and a desire to build is definitely important. The job is too physically demanding and financially unstable for you to be in it just for the money. Contrary to what many think, there is less money in high-end custom homebuilding—which is my market—than in production housing. Every house we do is a prototype, so there is much more time and detail involved.

hand who can fill in the knowledge gaps and supply the contacts you are missing.

If you are over sixty . . . Builders spend a lot of time on construction sites. However, there are a number of managerial and executive positions at large building companies. If you have experience in business, management, or accounting, you may want to consider applying for a high-level desk job at a building company.

Further Resources

The Builder is an online magazine that provides readers with useful advice and information on the home building industry. There are also helpful links to job sites.   http://www.builderonline.com
The Home Builders Institute maintains an excellent site that is a good resource for those interested in training programs and other educational opportunities in the home building field.   http://www.hbi.org
The **National Association of Home Builders** is a member-based trade organization that provides excellent networking opportunities as well as useful information on the building industry.   http://www.nahb.org

Urban Planner

Urban Planner

Career Compasses

Get your bearings on what it takes to become an urban planner.

Relevant Knowledge of computer databases and geographic information systems (GIS) as well as state legislations and zoning laws that pertain to urban and regional planning (30%)

Communication Skills to express your development plans clearly and generate interest from residents and government officials alike (30%)

Caring about a community's wellbeing and wanting to improve the quality of life for every citizen (20%)

Organizational Skills so that you can keep your notes, data, and reports in order while you are putting together plans and proposals (20%)

Destination: Urban Planner

From the grand boulevards of Paris to the parks movement of America, urban and regional planning is the driving force behind every great community. As the world's population has grown so too has the role of urban and regional planners. Nowadays, urban and regional planners are involved in all aspects of community development, from the construction of highways and airports to land conservation and economic development. It is an important job that can have far-reaching effects on a community's physical, social, and economic environment.

Although some urban and regional planners work for nonprofits or consulting firms, more than 50 percent are employed by local and state government agencies. Planners help government officials alleviate social, economic, and environmental problems by recommending locations for roads, schools, public housing, and other such infrastructure. While this may sound simple, the process of actually putting together a plan can be vexingly complex. Planners formulate ideas by meeting with residents, government officials, and special interest groups. They also use databases, spreadsheets, and a computerized system known as GIS (Geographic Information

Essential Gear

Understand research tools and programs.
Analyzing data is an important part of the planning process, so you should definitely be familiar with all the research programs that are used to collect data. The most commonly referenced is GIS, which is a software program that combines data and geographic mappings to analyze spatial information. Planners also use electronic poling systems, financial analysis spreadsheets, and demographic databases to conduct research and put together proposals.

Systems) to conduct research and analyze data. By combining all their data, research, and information collecting, planners are able to put together what is known as a master plan. The master plan—often hundreds of pages long—describes the present state of the community and proposes ways in which it could be improved. Some plans target one area of development, such as the creation of a bike lane, while others involve a more generalized plan of action. For example, if a city is in need of more commerce, urban planners might propose to redevelop the downtown area to include a public market or convention center.

Regardless of what a plan entails, government authorities need to approve a plan before it can be implemented. If there is even a whiff of public opposition—and there usually is—a plan can lose its momentum. In an effort to drum up public support, planners usually present their ideas to legislative committees, special interest groups, and neighborhood associations. Their presentations often include diagrams, aerial photos, maps, and lots of statistics.

Those who work in small private-sector companies or for sparsely populated regions typically handle all areas of planning and participate in most community meetings, whereas those who work for cities or large municipalities are typically assigned to an area of specialization, such as transportation planning, historic preservation, economic development, or parks and recreation. If you are passionate about a certain field, working at a large agency is a great way to effect change. However, those looking for an overview of the field should try working at a smaller agency where the responsibilities run high right away.

Whether you work in a bustling city or a sleepy town, the key to success in planning is caring about the community you live in and participating in local discourse. Although most planners clock a regular 40-hour week, their evenings are often spent at public hearings, town hall meetings, and other community activities.

Urban and regional planning is a multidisciplinary field that requires you to learn a wide range of skills sets. As a result, most government agencies ask that planners have a master's degree in urban or regional planning. There are a few schools that have acceptable bachelor's degree programs in urban planning, but without a master's degree it is very difficult to advance beyond an entry-level position.

Essential Gear

Learn the basics of a PowerPoint presentation. Planners are constantly giving presentations, so what better way to impress a prospective employer than by giving them a short PowerPoint presentation that highlights one of your planning ideas? Not only would a presentation show gumption and originality, it would also send a message that you are comfortable with public speaking and could handle the pressures of the job.

A master's degree in planning incorporates a variety of disciplines, including architecture, urban design, historic preservation, engineering, and the social sciences. Most programs are two years long and give students the opportunity to specialize in areas such as transportation planning, environmental and natural resources planning, and urban design. Planning programs also place an emphasis on community outreach. For example, the University of New Orleans has a community-based class project that focuses on rebuilding neighborhood economies in the aftermath of Hurricane Katrina.

Since urban planning incorporates many different areas of study, planning students come from a wide range of undergraduate backgrounds. Some enter master's programs with bachelor's degrees in economics and geography, while others major in creative writing or environmental studies. It is a field that values diverse interests and creative thinking.

The educational requirements for the job can be overwhelming, but the good news is that most programs provide you with internships and once you obtain your master's degree it is relatively easy to find employment in the field. In the past few decades the demand for sustainable living and better urban design has made planning a popular—and some might even say cool—profession.

You Are Here

Planning begins with a passion for change and a deep, abiding love for civic design.

Are you a creative thinker who works well with others? Urban planning is a collaborative field that requires teamwork and creative problem solving. A typical day might include a morning staff meeting to discuss plan management followed by an afternoon task meeting with engineers, architects, and health professionals. In order to succeed, you must be respectful of other people's ideas and able to communicate your own on both a visual and verbal level. The ideal planner is able to write reports and give speeches in addition to drawing maps and diagrams. It is a job that requires a lot of skill sets, but if you are good at spatial relations, enjoy working with people, and are passionate about creating change, this may be the job for you.

Do you have any experience in research or statistical analysis? In addition to strong visual and communication skills, planners should enjoy research and have an understanding of statistical analysis. Planners gather data from a variety of sources, including market research studies, census reports, and demographic databases. The research process can be grueling, however, the real difficulty lies in analysis. In order to discover trends in housing, population, and employment, you need to be gifted at statistical analysis. You also need to be comfortable with software programs such as GIS. Before committing yourself to the planning profession, you should take a course in computer science or statistics. If you enjoy the work, there is a good chance that planning is the right path for you.

Do you perform well under pressure? Planners often experience the pressures of deadlines and public speaking engagements. In addition, it is not uncommon for planners to receive political pressure from special

Navigating the Terrain

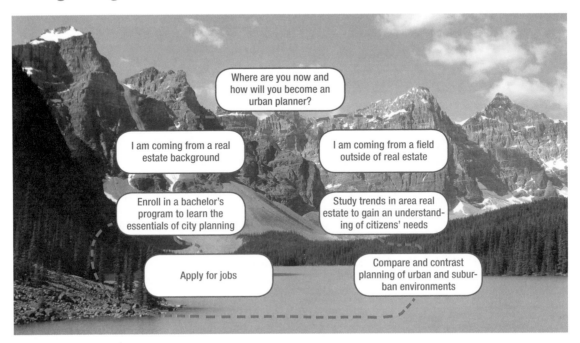

Where are you now and how will you become an urban planner?

I am coming from a real estate background

I am coming from a field outside of real estate

Enroll in a bachelor's program to learn the essentials of city planning

Study trends in area real estate to gain an understanding of citizens' needs

Apply for jobs

Compare and contrast planning of urban and suburban environments

interest groups. In order to succeed in this field, you need to be levelheaded and work well under pressure. The job comes with a lot of deadlines, disputes, and political drama, which is why it is important for planners to keep the big picture in mind and not be swayed by power or even popular opinion. Every group will have different needs and demands, and it is up to you to decide what ideas will best serve the community.

Organizing Your Expedition

Educate yourself before entering the world of planning.

Decide on a destination. In order to effectively plan a city or town, you have to be passionate about the community. Before choosing a job—or even a master's program—you ought to ask yourself whether you would like to work for a city, town, or suburb. Each environment has its merits. Planners employed by cities or larger municipalities get to work on large-scale projects, such as the development of a new highway or sports

Notes from the Field
Mark Pelligrini
Director of planning and economic development
Manchester, Connecticut

What were you doing before you got into municipal planning?

I had a bachelor's degree in journalism but I never could find work in that field. By chance, I was hired as a contract administrator in a county community development block grant office; from there, I was hired as a community relations coordinator in the same county. These two jobs exposed me to construction, engineering, urban and architectural design, policy and program planning, and the laws of zoning, subdivision, and building permitting.

Why did you decide to pursue a career in planning?

I like the interdisciplinary nature of the work. Planners need to be familiar with and work with experts in all sorts of fields, from policy development, politics, and the law to engineering, architecture, and urban design. One of the greatest parts about being a planner is having the ability to direct positive change in a community and improve people's lives. It is a very dynamic field.

stadium, though regional planners tend to have a greater say in matters and can initiate their own development plans—albeit on a smaller scale. Another question to consider is whether you would like to work for a private sector company. An increasing number of architecture, engineering, and technical consulting companies are hiring planners. The salaries and benefits at these private sector companies are often greater, but ultimately you are serving a company's needs and not those of the general public.

Scout the terrain. Picking a master's degree program can be bewildering, not to mention expensive, which is why it is important to find a program that suits your interests. Some schools have strong urban design departments, while others are big on natural resource development. If you can identify one or two subjects that you are passionate about, it will help you narrow down your school search. Another factor to consider is

What was involved in terms of education and training?

I realized that if I wanted to pursue a career in planning I needed to receive more training. I obtained a master's degree in urban and regional planning from the University of Pittsburgh. This was an important step for two reasons. 1) Combining a master's degree with my (then) level of experience allowed me to move into actual planning as opposed to administrative jobs, and 2) it gave me the opportunity to apply for management positions. Education is very important in this profession. Planners should pursue continuing education throughout their career. It is the only way to keep abreast of emerging trends, the latest technology, and new policy analysis and research on matters affecting cities and regions.

What are the keys to success as an urban or regional planner?

Analytical skills and the ability to communicate effectively are critical in this field. Successful planners understand that planning is a process that involves many different people and interests. In the public sector especially, planners needs to plan with people and not for people. They need to be transactional and flexible as opposed to rigid and dogmatic. The best way for planners to make themselves valuable to organizations or communities is to make sure plans actually happen. People appreciate and benefit from results, not from plans alone.

the school's location. Is it situated in an area that you could see yourself living or working in? Planning programs place a strong emphasis on local planning issues and many even require you to intern at local planning agencies, so it is a good idea to research a school's surrounding area and see if the environment stimulates you.

Find the path that's right for you. As a planner, you can create plans and programs that will have a positive impact on local issues such as pollution control, land preservation, and sheltering the homeless. It is a job that requires you to be a tireless advocate on behalf of a cause, which is why employers look for people who are passionate about certain subjects, be it environmental, economic, or social. Although there are many areas in which you can specialize, it should be noted that in recent years there has been a growing demand in both the public and private sector for environmental resource planners. If you are interested in protecting ecologically sensitive regions and putting caps on the amount of carbon monoxide emissions, then you should start taking courses in environmental studies.

Landmarks

If you are in your twenties . . . Now is the time to enroll in a good bachelor's or master's degree program. Urban planning is a vast field and there is much literature to read, so you can never start too early. Once you have enrolled in a degree program, find an internship at a local planning agency.

If you are in your thirties or forties . . . After a few years on the job, you will be given your own assignments, such as designing the physical layout of a large development. If you are a social creature with ambition to burn, you might want to start vying for the position of community planning director. It is a prestigious post that pays well and requires you to meet with officials and supervise a staff.

If you are in your fifties . . . Chances are you are ready for a change of pace. If so, you might want to consider a transfer to a larger jurisdiction with more complex problems and greater responsibilities.

If you are over sixty . . . If you have experience in planning and want to take on a leadership role, you should ask to be promoted to a higher position, such as director of community or economic planning. If, on the other hand, you are relatively new to the field, you should familiarize yourself with it. Consider reading such seminal texts as Alexander Garvin's *The American City: What Works and What Does Not* or Charles Holch's *The Practice of Local Government Planning*.

Further Resources

The **American Planning Association** is a membership organization that provides vital industry information to planning students as well as practicing planners. It also offers a list of accredited degree programs. http://www.planning.org

Planetizen is an excellent public-interest site that provides up-to-date urban planning news, commentary, book reviews, and job listings. http://www.planetizen.com

The **Regional Planning Association** is one of the most established regional planning associations in the nation. Although it only serves the Connecticut, New York, and New Jersey region, the Web site gives you clear insight into how plans are researched, designed, and implemented. http://www.rpa.org

Appraiser - - - - - - - - - - - - - - - - -

Appraiser

Career Compass

Get your bearings on what it takes to become an appraiser.

Relevant Knowledge of different appraisal techniques as well as a strong understanding of a particular region's property values (30%)

Organizational Skills to keep track of property maps, digital photos, tax assessments, and written reports (30%)

Mathematical Skills to use computer database programs, value homes, and put together estimates and tax assessments (30%)

Communication Skills enable you to write detailed reports, and when necessary, explain or defend the accuracy of your property estimates (10%)

Destination: Appraiser

The value of any given piece of real estate is determined by an appraisal, which is the process of estimating the selling price of a property under current market conditions. In simpler terms, this means that a real estate appraiser or assessor's job is to inspect properties and determine their current market value. It is absorbing work that requires a keen sense of observation and strong analytical skills. In addition to understanding how the real estate market works, appraisers and assessors must also have an encyclopedic knowledge of the region in which they work.

In order to estimate the fair value of a property, appraisers and assessors begin by visiting a property and talking with the residents. They then measure the property's square footage, determine the lot size and street frontage, and inspect the design and condition of the property's interior and exterior. Once the inspection is complete, real estate appraisers have to take a number of other factors into consideration before arriving at an estimate. They will typically look at lease records, previous appraisals, recent property sales in the area, and any construction or real estate trend that could influence the future value of a property.

Essential Gear

Have the right tools for appraisal. No appraiser or assessor should leave home without their tools, which typically include a camera, measuring tape, appraisal forms, and a GPS or street map. Nowadays, appraisers are using some high-tech tools to measure and record their findings, but there are still some who prefer the tried and true notebook and pencil. Regardless of what tools you decide to use, it is important to keep your tools organized and to have them with you at all times.

Once all the appropriate information has been gathered, appraisers and assessors write a detailed report that states the estimated value of the property and provides the research and reasoning to support their conclusions. Nowadays many reports include digital photos of the house as well as electronic maps of the surrounding area and its property distribution.

Although appraisers and assessors use similar appraisal techniques to arrive at their property estimates, the nature of their work differs significantly. An assessor is employed by the local government and is responsible for valuing properties exclusively for tax assessment purposes. The job requires a deep understanding of tax assessment procedures. Typically, assessors assess or reassess all the properties in a town or county on an annual or biannual basis, which can be grueling work. In addition, assessors are also responsible for dealing with property owners who contest their assigned property taxes, so they need to be able to defend their property assessments, either to the property owner or at a public hearing.

The number of staff employed by an assessor's office varies depending on the size of the local government. For example, a county office might employ up to 10 assessors, whereas a small town is likely to employ only one. Regardless of the office size, most assessors work standard hours and receive a steady salary.

Appraisers, on the other hand, have a more varied line of work. They could be asked to set a sales price, aid in a divorce settlement, or value a property for the purpose of a loan, investment, or mortgage. Those working in commercial appraisal also have the option of specializing in a particular area of real estate, such as office buildings or strip malls. The work is indeed varied, but oftentimes the hours can be rough, and appraisers—particularly those who are self-employed—often work weekends. Self-employed appraisers, often referred to as independent fee appraisers, typically work from home or a small office. Most appraisers—regardless of where they work—receive the bulk of their business from mortgage lenders, who need an estimate of a property's value before they can finalize any loan application process.

Whether you work as a real estate appraiser or assessor, the job requires a love of real estate and a lot of research and analysis. It is an active job that requires you to travel from inspection to inspection, so if you are looking for a simple desk job, this may not be the career for you. If, however, you enjoy writing reports and want a job that keeps you active, appraisal and assessing may be a good fit.

Essential Gear

Carry a laptop. If you want to impress your clients and cut down on your work time, you should bring a laptop to your work sites. Not only does it make the note-taking process faster and easier, you are also able to access data libraries, download images, and write your report on-site.

The first step toward becoming a state-certified appraiser or assessor is to obtain a bachelor's degree, preferably in a related field such as finance or real estate. As of 2008, most states now require a bachelor's degree or its equivalent in order to become a practicing appraiser and assessor. Unfortunately, there are no degree programs in appraisal, so once you have a bachelor's, you need to complete approximately 90 hours of classroom work and take a trainee license exam. Once you have your trainee license, you are required to train with a company or independent fee appraiser for 2,000 hours to get your regular license. Some states require you to take yet more classes and an additional exam in order to become state certified. Every state has different rules regarding licensing, so be sure to check before signing up for any courses or exams. For information on licensing, go to the Appraisal Foundation Web site at Appraisalfoundation.org. For state requirements, call your state appraisal regulatory agency.

The qualifications for assessors also vary by state but are usually similar to the requirements for an appraiser. In fact, many assessors become certified appraisers and then go on to take an additional exam or certification course for assessing. To find out your state's requirements, contact your local chapter of International Association of Assessing Officers.

You Are Here

Set yourself on the path to becoming an appraiser.

Have you had any experience working in real estate, appraisal, or banking? If you do not have any experience in real estate, take a clerical job at a real estate agency or appraisal office before enrolling in any expensive courses or certificate programs. Another alternative is to work at a brokerage firm or bank. Oftentimes, new appraisers feel intimidated by bankers or brokers who typically want a higher value for a property than it is worth. If you have experience working in the world of banking or brokering, you will be better equipped to handle the pressures of the job.

Are you familiar with a particular region's property values? Being an expert in a specific area's real estate market is paramount to success in appraising. In order to determine a property's value, you need to know the value of all the properties in the surrounding area. Those who are familiar with a region and have contacts in the area should find work easily. Although there is a greater demand for appraisers in heavily populated regions, the competition can be stiff in cities and large suburbs. For those just starting out, it is better to find work in an area that you are familiar with and then graduate to a more populated region where the pay might be higher.

Could you be described as organized and unbiased? Appraisers and assessors spend a lot of time traveling from site to site, so it is important that their tools for appraisal are properly maintained and all of the data,

Navigating the Terrain

How will you become an appraiser?

Find a clerical or trainee job at a real estate or appraisal agency

Learn the basics of the field and acquire trainee license

Log appropriate number of hours to acquire full appraisal license

Continue work with private corporation or start your own appraisal busines

images, and maps collected are easy to access. Appraisers and assessors maintain an extensive database from which they are able to arrive at an estimate of value, but appraising is far from an exact science. A lot of what an appraiser does is interpreting data, so it is important for appraisers to be honest and unbiased in their approach. If you are a confident, observant, and organized person who is not easily swayed by other people's opinions, you could be a perfect fit for appraising.

Organizing Your Expedition

Get everything in order as you prepare to become an appraiser.

Decide on a destination. There are many facets to the field of appraisal, and it is important to take stock of all your options before jumping into the field. Some real estate appraisers exclusively evaluate residential properties, while others specialize in appraising commercial, rental, or agricultural property. Some appraisers choose private practice, while

Notes from the Field

Connie Sue Clark-Louderback
Certified residential appraiser, A 1 Appraisals, Inc.
Knoxville, Iowa

How did you get started as a real estate appraiser?

I was a new part-time realtor and started with a real estate office that also did appraisals. As I gained more experience, I felt that appraising would be a better fit for me, rather than selling real estate. I opened my own appraising business in 2002 and I have never looked back.

Why did you want to get into the field?

I had spent years in construction, so I felt that real estate appraisal would be a comfortable fit for me. The job also provides a steady paycheck and the possibility of striking out on your own, which appealed to me. I wanted a career that would allow me to open my own business before I turned fifty, thus I left a successful career in realty, took some courses, and started my training.

others work for private corporations or financial institutions. It is important to decide which type of appraisal best suits your interests, needs, and personality. Location is perhaps the most important factor to consider. As an appraiser, your line of work often depends on where you live. For example, if you live in the Midwest, you might want to consider specializing in farm and agricultural appraisal, while if you live in a large city, you are best focusing your attention on high-rises or factories.

Scout the terrain. The value of a property is largely dictated by outside factors, such as political actions, economic forces, environmental changes, and demographic trends. For this reason alone, it is important for both appraisers and assessors to keep up on politics in their local sector. For example, an influx in new industry will create new jobs, which in turn will bring new families to a community and increase the demand for real estate. Conversely, if an area loses a major employer or is hit with a severe hurricane, home values are likely to plummet. Having a strong understanding of local politics is particularly important for assessors,

How did you break in?

In Iowa, as in many other states, you are required to take approximately 200 hours of education and have 2,500 hours of work experience before taking the Certified Residential Appraiser Exam. After completing the exam, I was fortunate to find a supervisor appraiser who was able to take on the training of a new appraiser. In most states, a supervisor can only have a limited number of trainees. In Iowa this number is only two.

What are the keys for success as a real estate appraiser?

Appraising is not a nine to five job. Nor is it a job for the kind of person who likes to wear a suit and tie to work. Appraisers are constantly visiting dusty work sites and crawling into attics and other small spaces. Honesty, hard work, and a good understanding of USPAP (Uniform Standards of Professional Appraisal Practice) are essential to the job. Appraisers should also be comfortable working under deadlines and should know when they are not qualified to complete an assignment.

as they are government employees. Prospective assessors interested in local or state government positions should apply to their local civil service agency for further information.

Find the path that's right for you. Once you obtain your trainee license, most states require you to clock in at least 2,000 hours in training before you can obtain your actual appraisal license. Trainee jobs often pay and are the best way to gain hands-on experience in the field, so finding the right one is imperative. Each trainee is assigned to a supervising appraiser who teaches you the tricks of the trade and signs off on all of your work. As a trainee, you spend most of your time shadowing a supervisor. Those who work hard enough often parlay the trainee job into a full-time position, so be sure to research all the appraisal offices in the area and find one that's right for you. An important factor that is often overlooked in the decision process is location. Trainees spend a lot of time traveling from site to site, so it is best to find a mentor who lives or works close to your home.

Landmarks

If you are in your twenties . . . Now is the time to get your bachelor's degree. If you already have one, you should consider taking a clerical job at a real estate agency or appraisal office before signing up for any licensing courses or exams. Aspiring assessors should contact their local civil service agency for further information on government jobs.

If you are in your thirties or forties . . . After obtaining an appraisal or assessor's license and gaining some experience in the field, it is time to start thinking about upward mobility. Appraisers should decide whether they would like to start their own appraisal company, and assessors should start angling for senior positions.

If you are in your fifties . . . You have probably gained some experience in the field and are capable of taking on a leadership role. Qualified real estate appraisers are often promoted to senior appraisers or senior real estate analyst positions. Some appraisers may advance by becoming specialists in a particular kind of property, such as industrial or agricultural property.

If you are over sixty . . . If you are an experienced appraiser who is tired of running to and from inspections, you might want to consider a management position at a commercial bank. Conversely, if you are completely new to the field of appraisal, banks, appraiser's offices, and loan offices hire trainee appraisers. Not only is it a great way to gain experience in the field, you are also paid for your efforts. For those who have worked in related fields, you should reach out to any appraisers that you have worked with in the past.

Further Resources

The Appraisal Foundation is authorized by Congress as the source of appraisal standards and appraiser qualifications. It is an excellent resource for those just starting out as well as those with experience who just want to stay up-to-date. http://www.appraisalfoundation.org
The **International Association of Assessing Officers** is the premier source for education and research in the field of assessment administra-

tion, property appraisal, and property tax policy. The site also offers access to the largest assessment library in the world.   http://www.iaao.org
The **American Society of Appraisers** is a membership-based society that has excellent accreditation programs and a Web site that offers useful networking tools.   http://www.appraisers.org

Financial Analyst

Financial Analyst

Career Compasses

Get your bearings on what it takes to become a financial analyst.

Mathematical Skills to understand spreadsheets and be able to calculate profits using complicated financial models and formulas (40%)

Communication Skills to meet and interact with clients and potentially work with a team of other analysts (25%)

Ability to Manage Stress when working under strict deadlines, advising clients, and juggling multiple projects at once (25%)

Relevant Knowledge of the real estate market as well as financial investment strategies (10%)

Destination: Financial Analyst

Real estate financial analysts chart the current state of the real estate market and predict what is to come in the future. In this sense, they could be called the financial gurus of the real estate world. Developers, brokers, investment companies, and even banks rely on analysts to determine the potential risks and returns of real estate investments. If you are interested in the real estate market, enjoy number crunching, and feel comfortable giving advice to colleagues, this could be an excellent match for you.

Analysts write reports that chart real estate trends and make fore-casts of what is to come. Each report varies depending on the scale of the project, but most reports include detailed cost analyses, pro forma modeling, a list of public agency requirements, disposition analysis, and a summary of any zoning impacts or title issues that could occur. In addition to writing reports, analysts also manage real estate portfolios through the use of statistical analysis. For example, when a bank is considering buying or leasing a property, they want to know three things: how much the property is really worth; how much it will cost to renovate; and how much profit it could potentially generate. It is the analyst's job to answer these three questions. To do so, analysts spend a lot of time studying tax returns, financial statements, and market data. If the property seems like a solid invest-ment, analysts will then put together status reports and term sheets to ensure that all the target terms and deadlines needed for funding can be met. Depending on the project, analysts might also inspect the prop-erty to ensure that everything complies with the terms of agreements.

Essential Gear

Take a trip to Brooks Brothers. Most analyst jobs are in banking houses or financial-advising firms, which means putting on corporate attire and subscribing to corporate culture. If you wish to rise in the industry, you should invest in a nice suit and attend as many business events and conferences as possible. Most people in finance indulge in costly hobbies and high-priced attire, which can be difficult to keep up with, particularly for those just starting out. The old adage, "You have to spend some money to make money" certainly applies to the finance world, but if you work hard, a large payoff will come during bonus season.

There will never be a sure way to predict future property values, but a good analyst significantly increases a company's chances of turning a profit. The job requires you to be quick with numbers and adept at communicating with a variety of different corporate types. As a result of all these responsibilities, analysts often carry a lot of stress. How-ever, the work can be very engaging and the salary is significant. Ac-cording to a 2006 survey conducted by the Bureau of Labor Statistics, the median salary for a real estate analyst was over $65,000 a year, and seasoned analysts employed at large firms can earn over $100,000 per year.

If you succeed in this field, there is also the opportunity to expand into other areas of real estate, such as development, brokerage, or consulting. Many real estate analysts transition into real estate market analysis, and vice versa. The two jobs are similar, except market analysts work for real estate brokers or consulting firms, whereas financial analysts are typically employed by developers or banks. A market analyst spends their time analyzing a particular market area over a five-year, two-year, or six-month period to see if prices went up or down. Brokers turn to market analysts to help answer questions such as, "What should I build?" "Will people buy it?" and "How much can I sell my home for?"

To become a real estate analyst, you need to be familiar with both local and national real estate markets and regulations. You should also be well versed in statistical analysis and have experience with a variety of software packages, including ARGUS software. Since the job requires specific skill sets, most companies require their analysts to have prior experience in real estate or investment banking. Certain banks, brokerage houses, and investment firms offer in-house training for beginning financial analysts, however analysts are still expected to have a thorough understanding of corporate accounting, statistics, and lender terminology before applying to any analyst position.

Essential Gear

Get a Hewlett-Packard financial calculator. If you ever take a course in financial analysis, you will probably be asked to buy a Hewlett-Packard calculator. If you are serious about financial analysis, this is one of the best investments you can make. Although there are other calculators on the market, The Hewlett-Packard-10B II is the industry standard because of its durability and reasonable cost. To wit, many analysts still use the same HP calculator that they had in college.

Although there are no official degree requirements for financial analysis, most aspirants have a bachelor's degree in finance, accounting, business, real estate, or a similar field. In recent years, due to an increase in the number of job applicants with college degrees, many prospective analysts are now applying for master's degrees in areas such as business administration. Although an MBA will certainly make you look good on paper, it is also helpful to have experience in other fields such as marketing, sales, or computer science.

You Are Here

Do some self-analysis to see if this is the right job for you.

Are you good at math and handy with a computer? Real estate analysis is all about crunching numbers and putting together presentations, which means you will be spending a lot of time with Microsoft Office, particularly Excel. Future analysts should enjoy working with computers, be comfortable preparing spreadsheets, and have experience with statistical analysis. Most employers prefer to hire people with backgrounds in computer science, math, or economics, but if you demonstrate an ability to understand and work with numbers, there is always the potential to excel as a real estate analyst.

Do you have strong communication skills? The title financial analyst is somewhat of a misnomer because so much of the job depends on presentation. Although written and oral presentations are a large part of

Navigating the Terrain

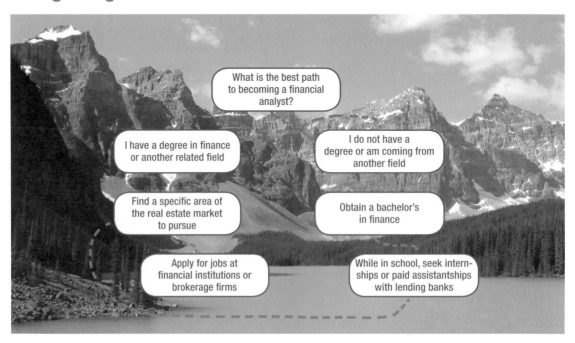

What is the best path to becoming a financial analyst?

I have a degree in finance or another related field

I do not have a degree or am coming from another field

Find a specific area of the real estate market to pursue

Obtain a bachelor's in finance

Apply for jobs at financial institutions or brokerage firms

While in school, seek internships or paid assistantships with lending banks

the job, analysts should also appear presentable. A large part of the job is conveying your research in a clear and convincing manner. You must be able to work well with other financial, legal, and asset management professionals. A good analyst is also a good listener and can choose his or her words carefully.

Are you a problem solver who works well under pressure? As an analyst, your job is to minimize a client's risk and maximize their return. Investors depend on you to create financial models and determine if a deal is feasible or if there is the potential to restructure. In addition to being responsible, an analyst needs to be able to evaluate a situation quickly. Multitasking is integral to the job. Aspirants must be able to handle a heavy workload, prioritize and complete work under strict deadlines, work as part of a team, and make big decisions under tight deadlines.

Organizing Your Expedition

Take the necessary steps to prepare yourself for a career in financial analysis.

Decide on a destination. If you are serious about becoming an analyst, the best opportunity available for those still in school is a summer analyst position at a bank that specializes in commercial real estate lending. Summer analyst positions are a great way to gain exposure to analytical business strategies and corporate culture. If, however, you do not want to work in a large corporate environment, consider working at a smaller real estate firm. Many commercial firms hire financial analysts to manage their real estate portfolios. Finally, there is market analysis, which involves researching specific real estate markets to assess market demand, potential for demand, and competitiveness of comparable properties in the area. This job requires you to have knowledge of specific markets, so if you have a particular area of real estate that interests you, this could be the job for you.

Scout the terrain. As an aspiring real estate analyst, it is a good idea to keep abreast of news stories, market movements, and industry profiles in financial newspapers and magazines. You should also familiarize yourself with ARGUS software, which is the industry standard for real estate

Notes from the Field

Daniel Hussey
Market analyst, PrimeTime Communities
Littleton, Massachusetts

What were you doing before you got into financial analysis?

I was working as a community planner for a consulting company. Prior to that, I worked as an assistant planner for a large municipality.

Why did you decide to pursue a career in real estate analysis?

I was attracted to real estate because I found it exciting. I felt there was a lot of opportunity to use my skills and experience in a unique way. Being an analyst can be a mix of sales and marketing, research, design, appraisal, and development.

How did you make the transition?

I stepped into the position with research experience and strong computer skills, which is a must. As far as training was concerned, it was more of a trial-by-fire process, but I did have a mentor who walked me through the research and presentation process. The transition was pretty easy once I had an understanding of the client's needs and the company's goals.

What are the keys to success as a real estate financial analyst?

First, strong communication skills. Real estate analysts have to deliver answers to very big questions, so you should be able to write convincing reports and deliver clear and precise presentations. Second, your research has to be valid and reliable. Your findings will be used to make very expensive decisions, so it is important to be accurate and thorough. Third, you have to be good at multitasking. At times, you will be working from two computers, two phones, and three e-mail accounts.

development and analysis. ARGUS has several programs, the most popular of which forecasts cash flows and values for real estate properties in a variety of markets. In addition to ARGUS, analysts also use PowerPoint and Excel on an almost daily basis, so a thorough understanding of these two programs is critical.

Find the path that's right for you. Long hours, low base pay, and a fair amount of responsibility characterize most entry-level positions in finance. Analysts pore through documents and work on teams that are abruptly rotated. The burnout rate is high, but if you can withstand two years at a financial institution, you will be prepared for almost any real estate analysis position. If you cannot find a job in finance, working at a brokerage firm will expose you to a different—and equally important—side of real estate analysis. At a brokerage firm you will learn all the necessary lender terminology and gain experience with commercial loans, both of which are integral to real estate analysis.

Landmarks

If you are in your twenties . . . The best thing you can do is get a college degree, preferably in a field related to financial analysis. College placement offices often help students find internships or jobs in financial analysis. In addition, certain corporations and brokerage firms send representatives to colleges for recruiting purposes.

If you are in your thirties or forties . . . You should start shooting for an associate or senior analyst ranking. Alternatively, if you are unhappy with your employment situation, many analysts choose to take a break during these years and pursue a master's degree.

Essential Gear

Read the *Wall Street Journal*. Not only is this the nation's leading business newspaper, it is also one of the best places to find classified ads for financial analyst positions. Firms from all parts of the country place job ads, so you should definitely pick up a copy if you are looking for employment. The *Wall Street Journal* is also a great way to keep up on business news and help improve your financial vocabulary.

If you are in your fifties . . . You might want to consider striking out on your own. If you enjoy the more interpersonal side of finance, why not start a management or consulting firm where you can use your people skills as well as your financial skills?

If you are over sixty . . . If you have already enjoyed a certain degree of success in finance, now is the time to transition into an executive or vice-presidential position within the company. If, on the other hand, you are completely new to the field but have a background in either real estate or finance, you probably have contacts in the field that could help you along. There are online courses offered on the subject of financial analysis. This can be a great way to learn the field without even leaving your home.

Further Resources

CCIM Institute is the world's largest commercial real estate brokerage network. Not only is CCIM a great networking site, it also offers certified classes in financial analysis, market analysis, and other aspects of commercial investment.   http://www.ccim.com

Principles of Finance with Excel by Simon Benninga is the perfect primer if you have never used Excel or are confused by the program.

Commercial Investment Real Estate **magazine** is run by the CCIM Institute and is a great source for industry news. All aspiring analysts should bookmark their page.   http://www.ciremagazine.com

Building Inspector

Building Inspector

Career Compasses

Get your bearings on what it takes to become a building inspector.

Relevant Knowledge of building inspection, including all aspects of the construction trade (30%)

Caring about the safety of buildings and the all the occupants who live and dwell in them (25%)

Mathematical Skills to understand, compute, and review construction plans, specifications, and other documents (25%)

Organizational Skills to keep blueprints and reports in order when traveling to and from construction and building inspections (20%)

Destination: Building Inspector

Building inspectors make sure that the structures we live and work in are safe to inhabit. Whether it is a structurally unsound balcony or a crack in the wall, it is the building inspector's job to identify what's wrong, file a report, and make sure that the problem is fixed in a timely manner. Not many people realize it, but building inspectors perform an important civic duty and are an integral part of the American workforce.

As a building inspector, you are responsible for overseeing a building before it is built, as it is being built, and after construction is completed. To give you an example, before builders can even break ground, a building inspector must make sure that the ground is stable and that all the blueprints comply with zoning regulations. In addition to construction worksites, inspectors also examine preexisting buildings to see if they comply with building codes and safety regulations. In particular, inspectors are responsible for upholding fire safety. A good inspector routinely checks fire sprinklers and alarm systems to see if they are functioning properly. Additionally, those who live in areas predisposed to severe weather conditions or natural disasters are required to enforce specific safety regulations.

On paper, the job can sound somewhat perfunctory, but in fact being a building inspector involves a lot of travel and excitement. One day you might drive two hours to investigate a construction site that does not have proper building permits, and another day you might be asked to inspect the new rooftop lighting system at the Sears Tower. The work is as interesting as it is important to the city and the public.

To determine whether a building is in good standing, inspectors use tape measures, survey instruments, metering devices, and equipment such as concrete strength measurers. Many bring a camera in case they need to document their findings, and all inspectors keep a log of their work. When inspectors discover a violation of a code or regulation, they must write a report and contact the contractor, superintendent, or supervisor in charge. If the problem is not fixed within a reasonable or otherwise specified period, most inspectors have authority to issue a "stop-work" order.

Essential Gear

In this profession, being certifiable is a good thing. Even if your employer does not require a lot of certifications, it is important to be certified in two or more areas of building inspection. Most building inspectors have the certified building official (CBO) certification, however, there are many other specialized certifications that will prepare you for a career in building inspection and set you apart from the competition. Here are some examples of specialized certifications: the qualified elevator inspector (QEI), certified fire protection specialist (CFPS), medical gas inspector (MGI), and residential building inspector (RBI). These certifications not only prove your technical expertise, they can also increase your earning potential and lead to better opportunities down the road.

Approximately half of the building inspectors in the United States are employed by local government agencies, such as municipal or county building departments. The remaining 50 percent are either self-employed or work for architectural and engineering services firms. Government agencies in cities and large municipalities have large inspection staffs that often include specialists in areas such as structural steel, reinforced concrete, electrical, and elevator inspection; whereas those who work for small firms or have their own businesses tend to work independently.

In recent years, there has been a major spike in the number of home inspectors, which is a relatively new addition to the century-old building and safety inspection profession. A home inspector is hired by a prospective homebuyer to conduct an inspection on a potential house, condo, or commercial building. Most home inspectors are self-employed and nearly all of them work in areas with moderate to expensive real estate. Their job is to look for and report violations of building codes. Unlike government inspectors, however, home inspectors do not have the power to enforce said codes. Since their responsibilities are not as great, the requirements for becoming a home inspector are not as strenuous.

Essential Gear

Bring your own inspection tools. It looks very organized and professional to bring your own equipment and tools to work, but if you really want to make a good impression, use a laptop for inspections. Your employer will probably provide you with notebooks and files, but laptops are a more organized and efficient way to file reports. Your boss is sure to take notice when you e-mail your reports from the actual site you are inspecting.

Although the educational requirements for building and home inspectors are minimal, there are several different requirements that building inspectors must fulfill before gaining entrance into the field. First off, most states require you to have at least two to three years of experience in a construction trade, such as carpentry, plumbing, or electrical work. If you do not have a background in construction, it can be hard to learn the ropes, which is why most regions have apprenticeship programs that combine paid on-the-job training with related classroom instruction.

Apprenticeship programs are a great introduction to building inspection, but there are other ways to gain entrance into the field. Government agencies often consider associate's or bachelor's degrees as a substitute for previous experience. Employers ideally look for candidates with four-year degrees in engineering or architecture, but you can also enter the field with a certificate or associate's degree in physics, drafting, or building inspection technology.

Once you have had a combination of classroom and on-the-job experience, it is time to take a license exam. Every state has a different policy regarding licenses and exams. Some states have individual licensing programs that inspectors must pass, while others require inspectors to obtain several certifications from associations such as the International

Essential Gear
Visit your local library. It may not seem like an essential tool at first, but your local library is a great place to go when your are job hunting. Many public libraries have government job listings, and if you have not taken your license or certification exam yet, your library should have a decent supply of books on construction and building inspection.

Code Council and the National Fire Protection Association. Before you start hitting the code books, contact the appropriate state agency to find out what requirements you must meet.

You Are Here

Prepare a new career trajectory for yourself.

Are you a physically active person who enjoys travel? Although the job does not require any heavy physical activity, examining buildings can be surprisingly exhausting. Building inspectors spend a lot of time climbing stairs, riding on platform hoists, and crouching to examine electrical sockets. It is an active job that requires you to be in decent shape. In addition, you have to enjoy the travel lifestyle. In most cases inspectors have scheduled inspections with buildings in nearby areas, though construction inspectors who are assigned to large-scale construction projects can be away from home for several weeks or more. Either way, the job requires a lot of driving, which means that you must have a driver's license and enjoy traveling to new places.

Do you have any experience in construction trades? Building inspection requires a wide range of technical expertise, which is why most inspectors are certified in several areas of construction. Before you take any exams or certification programs, it is important to gain experience in the field. Many inspectors have previously worked as carpenters, electricians, plumbers, or maintenance and repair workers. If you would rather go straight into building inspection, some building inspection associations offer assistant positions. This is another good way to get to know the field and see whether building inspection is right for you.

Are you a principled and strong-minded person? Apart from technical skills, this job requires a person of strong morals who can uphold rules. Oftentimes, landlords and builders will try to bribe, charm, or even threaten you into giving them a good report, which is why it is important that you take the job seriously. Honesty, candor, and conviction are just some of the characteristics that employers look for in a building inspector. Building inspectors do not win any popularity contests, but they do perform an important and valuable service.

Organizing Your Expedition

It takes more than just a tape measurer to make it as a building inspector.

Decide on a destination. The license and training requirements for government-employed versus self-employed building inspectors are radically different, so deciding which career path is right for you early on will save you a lot of time and energy. Government inspectors typically have to fulfill more requirements than self-employed inspectors; however, working for the government provides a steady salary and excellent benefits. Self-employed inspectors, on the other hand, work for themselves and have the potential to make a lot of money, but their hours tend to be longer and there is no a guarantee of a payoff at the end of the day. It is a matter of taste: If you are someone who likes to work in large office environments and cannot deal with the stress of running your own business, a government job would probably be a nice fit. If you have an entrepreneurial spirit and cannot stand corporate environments, working freelance for an architecture firm or starting your own home inspection business may be just the ticket.

Navigating the Terrain

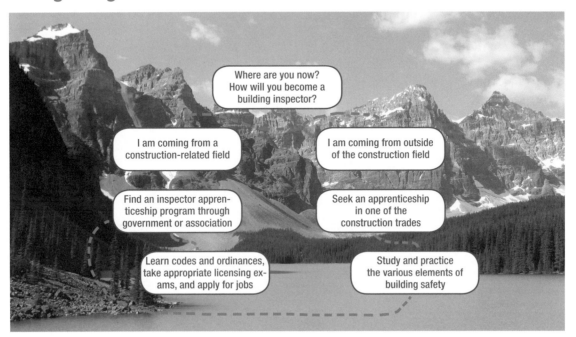

Where are you now? How will you become a building inspector?

I am coming from a construction-related field

I am coming from outside of the construction field

Find an inspector apprenticeship program through government or association

Seek an apprenticeship in one of the construction trades

Learn codes and ordinances, take appropriate licensing exams, and apply for jobs

Study and practice the various elements of building safety

Scout the terrain. Once you have decided where you would like to work, it is important to learn the area's particular building and safety codes and make sure you are up to speed on current inspection methods. If you have decided to work for the government, contact the building department of your city or county government to find out about programs in your area. Those interested in starting their own business should contact a veteran building inspector in the area. Oftentimes a veteran inspector can give you helpful tips, such as what sort of liability insurance to get and who to avoid in local politics.

Find the path that's right for you. Much of what a building inspector does can be learned on the job, which is why so many states require a minimum of two to three years of experience in a construction trade. Most community colleges and a lot of construction associations offer apprenticeship programs for those just starting out because most programs provide paid on-the-job experience and give you academic instruction.

Notes from the Field
Erik I. Hansen
Historic homes inspector
Lenexa, Kansas

What were you doing before you got into building inspection?

I had worked in museums and historic sites since high school, and my college education was geared toward pursuing that field. After nearly 20 years in public programming and exhibit work, I found that without an advanced degree, my options were limited for advancement and only lateral moves were available. I had no interest in returning to college for another two years.

Why did you decide to pursue a career in building inspection?

A family friend started a franchise of a property inspection company in 1992. He had recently decided to scale back and then retire. He was looking to sell the company, which was near Kansas City, but a previous arrangement to do so had just fallen through. I wanted to return to the Kansas City area, so he offered to take me on. In 2001, he turned the reins entirely over to me.

You will learn about contract specifications, inspection techniques, codes, ordinances, and regulations. There are many employers, employer associations, and joint labor-management organizations that sponsor apprenticeship programs. Additionally, some government agencies will allow you to shadow an experienced inspector. To find out what opportunities are available in your area, contact the American Construction Inspectors Association or your local community college.

Landmarks

If you are in your twenties . . . You should be doing everything you can to widen your field of expertise. This is the perfect age to have an apprenticeship in one of the construction trades. If you can find a mentor to show you the ropes and help you build contacts, then you will be in good shape for the future.

How did you make the transition?

The franchise provided three weeks of schooling and had a ride-along program, which basically meant that you shadowed an experienced inspector. Fortunately, I was able to bypass all of this because I already knew my boss and he mentored me through the process. I accompanied him on inspections for two years and then gradually assumed more responsibilities until I was running the business. Eventually, he stepped back, and I officially purchased the business in 2005.

What are the keys to success as a building inspector?

In this industry hard work brings success. Income is very much related to effort. If you are a self-employed inspector like myself, networking is also essential. Not enough good things can be said about the ability to network and get your name out there among realtors, mortgage brokers, and the service trades. Unfortunately, inspectors who do not work for the government or a large firm do not have a brand or company reputation to fall back on. Since I am not a part of a larger team, my clients regard me as an individual, which can be both good and bad. I have to do more PR work for the business, but I get to do so on my own clock. Moreover, I am able to create my own brand and image, which is nice.

If you are in your thirties or forties . . . If you have any experience in carpentry, plumbing, or electrical work, you will probably have an easy time with the license and certification exams. With your experience level, you should definitely be able to find work as an assistant building inspector. This is a great way to test out the job and see if it is right for you.

If you are in your fifties . . . If you have been working in a related field, you should develop an expertise in a particular area of construction or business inspection. For example, people who are familiar with the Americans with Disabilities Act have recently become a visible presence in building inspection agencies, as agencies need people to teach their staff about disability requirements.

If you are over sixty . . . If you have experience in a related field and have fulfilled your state's particular requirements for building inspectors, you should be able to work for a nongovernment agency. If you can find work on a contract basis, your schedule will be more flexible and you will not have to work as many hours.

Further Resources

The **International Code Council** is the gold standard for learning about building codes and safety regulations. In addition, their certification programs are among the best in the nation.   http://www.iccsafe.org

The **American Construction Inspectors Association** is one of the oldest membership-based associations in the nation and also one of the greatest sources for career and networking. Check out their job board. http://www.acia.com

The **National Fire Protection Association** is the authority on fire safety information and offers several different fire certification exams. http://www.nfpa.org

Appendix A

Going Solo: Starting Your Own Business

Starting your own business can be very rewarding—not only in terms of potential financial success, but also in the pleasure derived from building something from the ground up, contributing to the community, being your own boss, and feeling reasonably in control of your fate. However, business ownership carries its own obligations—both in terms of long hours of hard work and new financial and legal responsibilities. If you succeed in growing your business, your responsibilities only increase. Many new business owners come in expecting freedom only to find themselves chained tighter to their desks than ever before. Still, many business owners find greater satisfaction in their career paths than do workers employed by others.

The Internet has also changed the playing field for small business owners, making it easier than ever before to strike out on your own. While small mom-and-pop businesses such as hairdressers and grocery stores have always been part of the economic landscape, the Internet has made reaching and marketing to a niche easier and more profitable. This has made possible a boom in *microbusinesses*. Generally, a microbusiness is considered to have under ten employees. A microbusiness is also sometimes called a *SOHO* for "small office/home office."

The following appendix is intended to explain, in general terms, the steps in launching a small business, no matter whether it is selling your Web-design services or opening a pizzeria with business partners. It will also point out some of the things you will need to bear in mind. Remember also that the particular obligations of your municipality, state, province, or country may vary, and that this is by no means a substitute for doing your own legwork. Further suggested reading is listed at the end.

Crafting a Business Plan

It has often been said that success is 1 percent inspiration and 99 percent perspiration. However, the interface between the two can often be hard to achieve. The first step to taking your idea and making it reality is constructing a viable *business plan*. The purpose of a business plan is to think things all the way through, to make sure your ideas really are profitable, and to figure out the "who, what, when, where, why, and how" of your business. It fills in the details for three areas: your goals, why you think they are attainable, and how you plan to get to there. "You need to know where you're going before you take that first step," says Drew Curtis, successful Internet entrepreneur and founder of the popular newsfilter Fark.com.

Take care in writing your business plan. Generally, these documents contain several parts: An *executive summary* stating the essence of the plan; a *market summary* explaining how a need exists for the product and service you will supply and giving an idea of potential profitability by comparing your business to similar organizations; a *company description* which includes your products and services, why you think your organization will succeed, and any special advantages you have, as well as a description of *organization* and *management*; and your *marketing and sales strategy*. This last item should include market highlights and demographic information and trends that relate to your proposal. Also include a *funding request* for the amount of start-up capital you will need. This is supported by a section on *financials*, or the sort of cash flow you can expect, based on market analysis, projection, and comparison with existing companies. Other needed information, such as personal financial history, résumés, legal documents, or pictures of your product, can be placed in *appendices*.

Use your business plan to get an idea of how much startup money is necessary and to discipline your thinking and challenge your preconceived notions before you develop your cash flow. The business plan will tell you how long it will take before you turn a profit, which in turn is linked to how long it will before you will be able to pay back investors or a bank loan—which is something that anyone supplying you with money will want to know. Even if you are planning to subsist on grants or you are not planning on investment or even starting a for-profit company, the discipline imposed by the business plan is still the first step to organizing your venture.

A business plan also gives you a realistic view of your personal financial obligations. How long can you afford to live without regular income? How are you going to afford medical insurance? When will your business begin turning a profit? How much of a profit? Will you need to reinvest your profits in the business, or can you begin living off of them? Proper planning is key to success in any venture.

A final note on business plans: Take into account realistic expected profit minus realistic costs. Many small business owners begin by underestimating start-ups and variable costs (such as electricity bills), and then underpricing their product. This effectively paints them into a corner from which it is hard to make a profit. Allow for realistic market conditions on both the supply and the demand side.

Partnering Up

You should think long and hard about the decision to go into business with a partner (or partners). Whereas other people can bring needed capital, expertise, and labor to a business, they can also be liabilities. The questions you need to ask yourself are:

☞ Will this person be a full and equal partner? In other words, are they able to carry their own weight? Make a full and fair assessment of your potential partner's personality. Going into business with someone who lacks a work ethic, or prefers giving directions to working in the trenches, can be a frustrating experience.

☞ What will they contribute to the business? For instance, a partner may bring in start-up money, facilities, or equipment. However, consider if this is enough of a reason to bring them on board. You may be able to get the same advantages in another way—for instance, renting a garage rather than working out of your partner's. Likewise, doubling skill sets does not always double productivity.

☞ Do they have any liabilities? For instance, if your prospective partner has declared bankruptcy in the past, this can hurt your collective venture's ability to get credit.

☞ Will the profits be able to sustain all the partners? Many start-up ventures do not turn profits immediately, and what little they do produce can be spread thin amongst many partners. Carefully work out the math.

Also bear in mind that going into business together can put a strain on even the best personal relationships. No matter whether it is family, friends, or strangers, keep everything very professional with written agreements regarding these investments. Get everything in writing, and be clear where obligations begin and end. "It's important to go into business with the right people," says Curtis. "If you don't—if it degrades into infighting and petty bickering—it can really go south quickly."

Incorporating. . . or Not

Think long and hard about incorporating. Starting a business often requires a fairly large—and risky—financial investment, which in turn exposes you to personal liability. Furthermore, as your business grows, so does your risk. Incorporating can help you shield yourself from this liability. However, it also has disadvantages.

To begin with, incorporating is not necessary for conducting professional transactions such as obtaining bank accounts and credit. You can do this as a sole proprietor, partnership, or simply by filing a DBA ("doing business as") statement with your local court (also known as "trading as" or an "assumed business name"). The DBA is an accounting entity that facilitates commerce and keeps your business' money separate from your own. However, the DBA does not shield you from responsibility if your business fails. It is entirely possible to ruin your credit, lose your house, and have your other assets seized in the unfortunate event of bankruptcy.

The purpose of incorporating is to shield yourself from personal financial liability. In case the worst happens, only the business' assets can be taken. However, this is not always the best solution. Check your local laws: Many states have laws that prevent a creditor from seizing a non-incorporated small business' assets in case of owner bankruptcy. If you are a corporation, however, the things you use to do business that are owned by the corporation—your office equipment, computers, restaurant refrigerators, and other essential equipment—may be seized by creditors, leaving you no way to work yourself out of debt. This is why it is imperative to consult with a lawyer.

There are other areas in which being a corporation can be an advantage, such as business insurance. Depending on your business needs, insurance can be for a variety of things: malpractice, against delivery failures or spoilage, or liability against defective products or accidents. Furthermore, it is easier to hire employees, obtain credit, and buy health insurance as an organization than as an individual. However, on the downside, corporations are subject to specific and strict laws concerning management and ownership. Again, you should consult with a knowledgeable legal expert.

Among the things you should discuss with your legal expert are the advantages and disadvantages of incorporating in your jurisdiction and which type of incorporation is best for you. The laws on liability and how much of your profit will be taken away in taxes vary widely by state and country. Generally, most small businesses owners opt for *limited liability companies* (LLCs), which gives them more control and a more flexible management structure. (Another possibility is a *limited liability partnership*, or *LLP*, which is especially useful for professionals such as doctors and lawyers.) Finally, there is the *corporation*, which is characterized by transferable ownerships shares, perpetual succession, and, of course, limited liability.

Most small businesses are sole proprietorships, partnerships, or privately-owned corporations. In the past, not many incorporated, since it was necessary to have multiple owners to start a corporation. However, this is changing, since it is now possible in many states for an individual to form a corporation. Note also that the form your business takes is usually not set in stone: A sole proprietorship or partnership can switch to become an LLC as it grows and the risks increase; furthermore, a successful LLC can raise capital by changing its structure to become a corporation and selling stock.

Legal Issues

Many other legal issues besides incorporating (or not) need to be addressed before you start your business. It is impossible to speak directly to every possible business need in this brief appendix, since regulations, licenses, and health and safety codes vary by industry and locality. A restaurant in Manhattan, for instance, has to deal not only with the usual issues such as health inspectors, and the state liquor board, but obscure regulations such as New York City's cabaret laws, which prohibit dancing without a license in a place where alcohol is sold. An asbestos-abatement company, on the other hand, has a very different set of standards it has to abide by, including federal regulations. Researching applicable laws is part of starting up any business.

Part of being a wise business owner is knowing when you need help. There is software available for things like bookkeeping, business plans, and Web site creation, but generally, consulting with a knowledgeable professional—an accountant or a lawyer (or both)—is the smartest move. One of the most common mistakes is believing that just because you have expertise in the technical aspects of a certain field, you know all about running a business in that field. Whereas some people may balk at the expense, by suggesting the best way to deal with possible problems, as well as cutting through red tape and seeing possible pitfalls that you may not even have been aware of, such professionals usually more than make up for their cost. After all, they have far more experience at this than does a first-time business owner!

Financial

Another necessary first step in starting a business is obtaining a bank account. However, having the account is not as important as what you do with it. One of the most common problems with small businesses is undercapitalization—especially in brick-and-mortar businesses that sell or make something, rather than service-based businesses. The rule of thumb is that you should have access to money equal to your first year's anticipated profits, plus start-up expenses. (Note that this is not the same as having the money on hand—see the discussion on lines of credit, below.) For instance, if your annual rent, salaries, and equipment will cost $50,000 and you expect $25,000 worth of profit in your first year, you should have access to $75,000 worth of financing.

You need to decide what sort of financing you will need. Small business loans have both advantages and disadvantages. They can provide critical start-up credit, but in order to obtain one, your personal credit will need to be good, and you will, of course, have to pay them off with interest. In general, the more you and your partners put into the business yourselves, the more credit lenders will be willing to extend to you.

Equity can come from your own personal investment, either in cash or an equity loan on your home. You may also want to consider bringing on partners—at least limited financial partners—as a way to cover start-up costs.

It is also worth considering obtaining a line of credit instead of a loan. A loan is taken out all at once, but with a line of credit, you draw on the money as you need it. This both saves you interest payments and means that you have the money you need when you need it. Taking out too large of a loan can be worse than having no money at all! It just sits there collecting interest—or, worse, is spent on something utterly unnecessary—and then is not around when you need it most.

The first five years are the hardest for any business venture; your venture has about double the usual chance of closing in this time (1 out of 6, rather than 1 out of 12). You will probably have to tighten your belt at home, as well as work long hours and keep careful track of your business expenses. Be careful with your money. Do not take unnecessary risks, play it conservatively, and always keep some capital in reserve for emergencies. The hardest part of a new business, of course, is the learning curve of figuring out what, exactly, you need to do to make a profit, and so the best advice is to have plenty of savings—or a job to provide income—while you learn the ropes.

One thing you should not do is count on venture capitalists or "angel investors," that is, businesspeople who make a living investing on other businesses in the hopes that their equity in the company will increase in value. Venture capitalists have gotten something of a reputation as indiscriminate spendthrifts due to some poor choices made during the dot-com boom of the late 1990s, but the fact is that most do not take risks on unproven products. Rather, they are attracted to young companies that have the potential to become regional or national powerhouses and give better-than-average returns. Nor are venture capitalists endless sources of money; rather, they are savvy businesspeople who are usually attracted to companies that have already experienced a measure of success. Therefore, it is better to rely on your own resources until you have proven your business will work.

Bookkeeping 101

The principles of double-entry bookkeeping have not changed much since its invention in the fifteenth century: one column records debits, and one records credits. The trick is *doing* it. As a small business owner, you need to be disciplined and meticulous at recording your finances. Thankfully, today there is software available that can do everything from tracking payables and receivables to running checks and generating reports.

Honestly ask yourself if you are the sort of person who does a good job keeping track of finances. If you are not, outsource to a bookkeeping company or hire someone to come in once or twice a week to enter invoices and generate checks for you. Also remember that if you have employees or even freelancers, you will have to file tax forms for them at the end of the year.

Another good idea is to have an accountant for your business to handle advice and taxes (federal, state, local, sales tax, etc.). In fact, consulting with a certified public accountant is a good idea in general, since they are usually aware of laws and rules that you have never even heard of.

Finally, keep your personal and business accounting separate. If your business ever gets audited, the first thing the IRS looks for is personal expenses disguised as business expenses. A good accountant can help you to know what are legitimate business expenses. Everything you take from the business account, such as payroll and reimbursement, must be recorded and classified.

Being an Employer

Know your situation regarding employees. To begin with, if you have any employees, you will need an Employer Identification Number (EIN), also sometimes called a Federal Tax Identification Number. Getting an EIN is simple: You can fill out IRS form SS-4, or complete the process online at http://www.irs.gov.

Having employees carries other responsibilities and legalities with it. To begin with, you will need to pay payroll taxes (otherwise known as "withholding") to cover income tax, unemployment insurance, Social Security, and Medicare, as well as file W-2 and W-4 forms with the government. You will also be required to pay worker's compensation insurance, and will probably also want to find medical insurance. You are also required to abide by your state's nondiscrimination laws. Most states require you to post nondiscrimination and compensation notices in a public area.

Many employers are tempted to unofficially hire workers "off the books." This can have advantages, but can also mean entering a legal gray area. (Note, however, this is different from hiring freelancers, a temp employed by another company, or having a self-employed professional such as an accountant or bookkeeper come in occasionally to provide a service.) It is one thing to hire the neighbor's teenage son on a one-time basis to help you move some boxes, but quite another to have full-time workers working on a cash-and-carry basis. Regular wages must be noted in the accounts, and gaps may be questioned in the event of an audit. If the workers are injured on the job, you are not covered by worker's comp, and are thus vulnerable to lawsuits. If the workers you hired are not legal residents, you can also be liable for civil and criminal penalties. In general, it is best to keep your employees as above-board as possible.

Building a Business

Good business practices are essential to success. First off, do not overextend yourself. Be honest about what you can do and in what time frame. Secondly, be a responsible business owner. In general, if there is a problem, it is best to explain matters honestly to your clients than to leave them without word and wondering. In the former case, there is at least the possibility of salvaging your reputation and credibility.

Most business is still built by personal contacts and word of mouth. It is for this reason that maintaining your list of contacts is an essential practice. Even if a particular contact may not be useful at a particular moment, a future opportunity may present itself—or you may be able to send someone else to them. Networking, in other words, is as important when you are the boss as when you are looking for a job yourself. As the owner of a company, having a network means getting services on better terms, knowing where to go if you need help with a particular problem, or simply being in the right place at the right time to exploit an opportunity. Join professional organizations, the local Chamber of Commerce, clubs and community organizations, and learn to play golf. And remember—never burn a bridge.

Advertising is another way to build a business. Planning an ad campaign is not as difficult as you might think: You probably already know your media market and business community. The trick is applying it. Again, go with your instincts. If you never look twice at your local weekly, other people probably do not, either. If you are in a high-tourist area, though, local tourist maps might be a good way to leverage your marketing dollar. Ask other people in your area or market who have businesses similar to your own. Depending on your focus, you might want to consider everything from AM radio or local TV networks, to national trade publications, to hiring a PR firm for an all-out blitz. By thinking about these questions, you can spend your advertising dollars most effectively.

Nor should you underestimate the power of using the Internet to build your business. It is a very powerful tool for small businesses, potentially reaching vast numbers of people for relatively little outlay of money. Launching a Web site has become the modern equivalent of hanging out your shingle. Even if you are primarily a brick-and-mortar business, a Web presence can still be an invaluable tool—your store or offices will show up on Google searches, plus customers can find directions to visit you in person. Furthermore, the Internet offers the small-business owner many useful tools. Print and design services, order fulfillment, credit card processing, and networking—both personal and in terms of linking to other sites—are all available online. Web advertising can be useful, too, either by advertising on specialty sites that appeal to your audience, or by using services such as Google AdWords.

Amateurish print ads, TV commercials, and Web sites do not speak well of your business. Good media should be well-designed, well-edited, and well-put together. It need not, however, be expensive. Shop around and, again, use your network.

Flexibility is also important. "In general, a business must adapt to changing conditions, find new customers and find new products or services that customers need when the demand for their older products or services diminishes," says James Peck, a Long Island, New York, entrepreneur. In other words, if your original plan is not working out, or if demand falls, see if you can parlay your experience, skills, and physical plant into meeting other needs. People are not the only ones who can change their path in life; organizations can, too.

A Final Word

In business, as in other areas of life, the advice of more experienced people is essential. "I think it really takes three businesses until you know what you're doing," Drew Curtis confides. "I sure didn't know what I was doing the first time." Listen to what others have to say, no matter whether it is about your Web site or your business plan. One possible solution is seeking out a mentor, someone who has previously launched a successful venture in this field. In any case, before taking any step, ask as many people as many questions as you can. Good advice is invaluable.

Further Resources

American Independent Business Alliance
http://www.amiba.net

American Small Business League
http://www.asbl.com

IRS Small Business and Self-Employed One-Stop Resource
http://www.irs.gov/businesses/small/index.html

The Riley Guide: Steps in Starting Your Own Business
http://www.rileyguide.com/steps.html

Small Business Administration
http://www.sba.gov

Appendix B

Outfitting Yourself for Career Success

As you contemplate a career shift, the first component is to assess your interests. You need to figure out what makes you tick, since there is a far greater chance that you will enjoy and succeed in a career that taps into your passions, inclinations, natural abilities, and training. If you have a general idea of what your interests are, you at least know in which direction you want to travel. You may know you want to simply switch from one sort of nursing to another, or change your life entirely and pursue a dream you have always held. In this case, you can use a specific volume of The Field Guides to Finding a New Career to discover which position to target. If you are unsure of the direction you want to take, well, then the entire scope of the series is open to you! Browse through to see what appeals to you, and see if it matches with your experience and abilities.

The next step you should take is to make a list—do it once in writing—of the skills you have used in a position of responsibility that transfer to the field you are entering. People in charge of interviewing and hiring may well understand that the skills they are looking for in a new hire are used in other fields, but you must spell it out. Most job descriptions are partly a list of skills. Map your experience into that, and very early in your contacts with a prospective employer explicitly address how you acquired your relevant skills. Pick a relatively unimportant aspect of the job to be your ready answer for where you would look forward to learning within the organization, if this seems essentially correct. When you transfer into a field, softly acknowledge a weakness while relating your readiness to learn, but never lose sight of the value you offer both in your abilities and in the freshness of your perspective.

Energy and Experience

The second component in career-switching success is energy. When Jim Fulmer was 61, he found himself forced to close his piano-repair business. However, he was able to parlay his knowledge of music, pianos, and the musical instruments industry into another job as a sales representative for a large piano manufacturer, and quickly built up a clientele of musical-instrument retailers throughout the East Coast. Fulmer's experience highlights another essential lesson for career-changers: There are plenty of opportunities out there, but jobs will not come to you—especially the career-oriented, well-paying ones. You have to seek them out.

Jim Fulmer's case also illustrates another important point: Former training and experience can be a key to success. "Anyone who has to make a career change in any stage of life has to look at what skills they have acquired but may not be aware of," he says. After all, people can more easily change into careers similar to the ones they are leaving. Training and experience also let you enter with a greater level of seniority, provided you have the other necessary qualifications. For instance, a nurse who is already experienced with administering drugs and their benefits and drawbacks, and who is also graced with the personality and charisma to work with the public, can become a pharmaceutical company sales representative.

Unlock Your Network

The next step toward unlocking the perfect job is networking. The term may be overused, but the idea is as old as civilization. More than other animals, humans need one another. With the Internet and telephone, never in history has it been easier to form (or revive) these essential links. One does not have to gird oneself and attend reunion-type events (though for many this is a fine tactic)—but keep open to opportunities to meet people who may be friendly to you in your field. Ben Franklin understood the principle well—*Poor Richard's Almanac* is something of a treatise on the importance of cultivating what Franklin called "friendships" with benefactors. So follow in the steps of the founding fathers and make friends to get ahead. Remember: helping others feels good; it's often the receiving that gets a little tricky. If you know someone particularly well-connected in your field, consider tapping one or two less important connections first so that you make the most of the important one. As you proceed, keep your strengths foremost in your mind because the glue of commerce is mutual interest.

Eighty percent of job openings are *never advertised*, and, according to the U.S. Bureau of Labor statistics, more than half of all employees landed their jobs through networking. Using your personal contacts is far more efficient and effective than trusting your résumé to the Web.

On the Web, an employer needs to sort through tens of thousands—or millions—of résumés. When you direct your application to one potential employer, you are directing your inquiry to one person who already knows you. The personal touch is everything: Human beings are social animals, programmed to "read" body language; we are naturally inclined to trust those we meet in person, or who our friends and coworkers have recommended. While Web sites can be useful (for looking through help-wanted ads, for instance), expecting employers to pick you out of the slush pile is as effective as throwing your résumé into a black hole.

Do not send your résumé out just to make yourself feel like you're doing something. The proper way to go about things is to employ discipline and order, and then to apply your charm. Begin your networking efforts by making a list of people you can talk to: colleagues, coworkers, and supervisors, people you have had working relationship with, people from church, athletic teams, political organizations, or other community groups, friends, and relatives. You can expand your networking opportunities by following the suggestions in each chapter of the volumes. Your goal here is not so much to land a job as to expand your possibilities and knowledge: Though the people on your list may not be in the position to help you themselves, they might know someone who is. Meeting with them might also help you understand traits that matter and skills that are valued in the field in which you are interested. Even if the person is a potential employer, it is best to phrase your request as if you were seeking information: "You might not be able to help me, but do you know someone I could talk to who could tell me more about what it is like to work in this field?" Being hungry gives one impression, being desperate quite another.

Keep in mind that networking is a two-way street. If you meet someone who has an opening that is not right for you, but you could recommend someone else, you have just added to your list two people who will be favorably disposed toward you in the future. Also, bear in mind that *you* can help people in *your* old field, thus adding to your own contacts list.

Networking is especially important to the self-employed or those who start their own businesses. Many people in this situation begin because they either recognize a potential market in a field that they are familiar with, or because full-time employment in this industry is no longer a possibility. Already being well-established in a field can help, but so can asking connections for potential work and generally making it known that you are ready, willing, and able to work. Working your professional connections, in many cases, is the *only* way to establish yourself. A freelancer's network, in many cases, is like a spider's web. The spider casts out many strands, since he or she never knows which one might land the next meal.

Dial-Up Help

In general, it is better to call contacts directly than to e-mail them. E-mails are easy for busy people to ignore or overlook, even if they do not mean to. Explain your situation as briefly as possible (see the discussion of the "elevator speech"), and ask if you could meet briefly, either at their office or at a neutral place such as a café. (Be sure that you pay the bill in such a situation—it is a way of showing you appreciate their time and effort.) If you get someone's voicemail, give your "elevator speech" and then say you will call back in a few days to follow up—and then do so. If you reach your contact directly and they are too busy to speak or meet with you, make a definite appointment to call back at a later date. Be persistent, but not annoying.

Once you have arranged a meeting, prep yourself. Look at industry publications both in print and online, as well as news reports (here, GoogleNews, which lets you search through online news reports, can be very handy). Having up-to-date information on industry trends shows that you are dedicated, knowledgeable, and focused. Having specific questions on employers and requests for suggestions will set you apart from the rest of the job-hunting pack. Knowing the score—for instance, asking about the value of one sort of certification instead of another—pegs you as an "insider," rather than a dilettante, someone whose name is worth remembering and passing along to a potential employer.

Finally, set the right mood. Here, a little self-hypnosis goes a long way: Look at yourself in the mirror, and tell yourself that you are an enthusiastic, committed professional. Mood affects confidence and performance. Discipline your mind so you keep your perspective and self-respect. Nobody wants to hire someone who comes across as insincere, tells a sob story, or is still in the doldrums of having lost their previous job. At the end of any networking meeting, ask for someone else who might be able to help you in your journey to finding a position in this field, either with information or a potential job opening.

Get a Lift

When you meet with a contact in person (as well as when you run into anyone by chance who may be able to help you), you need an "elevator speech" (so-named because it should be short enough to be delivered during an elevator ride from a ground level to a high floor). This is a summary in which, in less than two minutes, you give them a clear impression of who you are, where you come from, your experience and goals, and why you are on the path you are on. The motto above Plato's Academy holds true: Know Thyself (this is where our Career Compasses and guides will help you). A long and rambling "elevator story" will get you nowhere. Furthermore, be positive: Neither a sad-sack story nor a tirade explaining how everything that went wrong in your old job is someone else's fault will get you anywhere. However, an honest explanation of a less-than-fortunate circumstance, such as a decline in business forcing an office closure, needing to change residence to a place where you are not qualified to work in order to further your spouse's career, or needing to work fewer hours in order to care for an ailing family member, is only honest.

An elevator speech should show 1) you know the business involved; 2) you know the company; 3) you are qualified (here, try to relate your education and work experience to the new situation); and 4) you are goal-oriented, dependable, and hardworking. Striking a balance is important; you want to sound eager, but not overeager. You also want to show a steady work experience, but not that you have been so narrowly focused that you cannot adjust. Most important is emphasizing what you can do for the company. You will be surprised how much information you can include in two minutes. Practice this speech in front of a mirror until you have the key points down perfectly. It should sound natural, and you should come across as friendly, confident, and assertive. Finally, remember eye contact! Good eye contact needs to be part of your presentation, as well as your everyday approach when meeting potential employers and leads.

Get Your Résumé Ready

Everyone knows what a résumé is, but how many of us have really thought about how to put one together? Perhaps no single part of the job search is subject to more anxiety—or myths and misunderstandings—than this 8 ½-by-11-inch sheet of paper.

On the one hand, it is perfectly all right for someone—especially in certain careers, such as academia—to have a résumé that is more than one page. On the other hand, you do not need to tell a future employer *everything*. Trim things down to the most relevant; for a 40-year-old to mention an internship from two decades ago is superfluous. Likewise, do not include irrelevant jobs, lest you seem like a professional career-changer.

Tailor your descriptions of your former employment to the particular position you are seeking. This is not to say you should lie, but do make your experience more appealing. If the job you're looking for involves supervising other people, say if you have done this in the past; if it involves specific knowledge or capabilities, mention that you possess these qualities. In general, try to make your past experience seem similar to what you are seeking.

The standard advice is to put your Job Objective at the heading of the résumé. An alternative to this is a Professional Summary, which some recruiters and employers prefer. The difference is that a Job Objective mentions the position you are seeking, whereas a Professional Summary mentions your background (e.g. "Objective: To find a position as a sales representative in agribusiness machinery" versus "Experienced sales representative; strengths include background in agribusiness, as well as building team dynamics and market expansion"). Of course, it is easy to come up with two or three versions of the same document for different audiences.

The body of the résumé of an experienced worker varies a lot more than it does at the beginning of your career. You need not put your education or your job experience first; rather, your résumé should emphasize your strengths. If you have a master's degree in a related field, that might want to go before your unrelated job experience. Conversely, if too much education will harm you, you might want to bury that under the section on professional presentations you have given that show how good you are at communicating. If you are currently enrolled in a course or other professional development, be sure to note this (as well as your date of expected graduation). A résumé is a study of blurs, highlights, and jewels. You blur everything you must in order to fit the description of your experience to the job posting. You highlight what is relevant from each and any of your positions worth mentioning. The jewels are the little headers and such—craft them, since they are what is seen first.

You may also want to include professional organizations, work-related achievements, and special abilities, such as your fluency in a foreign language. Also mention your computer software qualifications and capabilities, especially if you are looking for work in a technological field or if you are an older job-seeker who might be perceived as behind the technology curve. Including your interests or family information might or might not be a good idea—no one really cares about your bridge club, and in fact they might worry that your marathon training might take away from your work commitments, but, on the other hand, mentioning your golf handicap or three children might be a good idea if your potential employer is an avid golfer or is a family woman herself.

You can either include your references or simply note, "References available upon request." However, be sure to ask your references' permission to use their names and alert them to the fact that they may be contacted before you include them on your résumé! Be sure to include name, organization, phone number, and e-mail address for each contact.

Today, word processors make it easy to format your résumé. However, beware of prepackaged résumé "wizards"—they do not make you stand out in the crowd. Feel free to strike out on your own, but remember the most important thing in formatting a résumé is consistency. Unless you have a background in typography, do not get too fancy. Finally, be sure to have someone (or several people!) read your résumé over for you.

For more information on résumé writing, check out Web sites such as http://www.résumé.monster.com.

Craft Your Cover Letter

It is appropriate to include a cover letter with your résumé. A cover letter lets you convey extra information about yourself that does not fit or is not always appropriate in your résumé, such as why you are no longer working in your original field of employment. You can and should also mention the name of anyone who referred you to the job. You can go into some detail about the reason you are a great match, given the job description. Also address any questions that might be raised in the potential employer's mind (for instance, a gap in employment). Do not, however, ramble on. Your cover letter should stay focused on your goal: To offer a strong, positive impression of yourself and persuade the hiring manager that you are worth an interview. Your cover letter gives you a chance to stand out from the other applicants and sell yourself. In fact, according to a CareerBuilder.

com survey, 23 percent of hiring managers say a candidate's ability to relate his or her experience to the job at hand is a top hiring consideration.

Even if you are not a great writer, you can still craft a positive yet concise cover letter in three paragraphs: An introduction containing the specifics of the job you are applying for; a summary of why you are a good fit for the position and what you can do for the company; and a closing with a request for an interview, contact information, and thanks. Remember to vary the structure and tone of your cover letter—do not begin every sentence with "I."

Ace Your Interview

In truth, your interview begins well before you arrive. Be sure to have read up well on the company and its industry. Use Web sites and magazines—http://www.hoovers.com offers free basic business information, and trade magazines deliver both information and a feel for the industries they cover. Also, do not neglect talking to people in your circle who might know about trends in the field. Leave enough time to digest the information so that you can give some independent thought to the company's history and prospects. You don't need to be an expert when you arrive to be interviewed; but you should be comfortable. The most important element of all is to be poised and relaxed during the interview itself. Preparation and practice can help a lot.

Be sure to develop well-thought-through answers to the following, typical interview openers and standard questions.

☞ Tell me about yourself. (Do not complain about how unsatisfied you were in your former career, but give a brief summary of your applicable background and interest in the particular job area.) If there is a basis to it, emphasize how much you love to work and how you are a team player.

☞ Why do you want this job? (Speak from the brain, and the heart—of course you want the money, but say a little here about what you find interesting about the field and the company's role in it.)

☞ What makes you a good hire? (Remember here to connect the company's needs and your skill set. Ultimately, your selling points probably come down to one thing: you will make your employer money. You want the prospective hirer to see that your skills are valuable not to the world in general but to this specific company's bottom line. What can you do for them?)

☞ What led you to leave your last job? (If you were fired, still try to say something positive, such as, "The business went through a challenging time, and some of the junior marketing people were let go.")

Practice answering these and other questions, and try to be genuinely positive about yourself, and patient with the process. Be secure but not cocky; don't be shy about forcing the focus now and then on positive contributions you have made in your working life—just be specific. As with the elevator speech, practice in front of the mirror.

A couple pleasantries are as natural a way as any to start the actual interview, but observe the interviewer closely for any cues to fall silent and formally begin. Answer directly; when in doubt, finish your phrase and look to the interviewer. Without taking command, you can always ask, "Is there more you would like to know?" Your attentiveness will convey respect. Let your personality show too—a positive attitude and a grounded sense of your abilities will go a long way to getting you considered. During the interview, keep your cell phone off and do not look at your watch. Toward the end of your meeting, you may be asked whether you have any questions. It is a good idea to have one or two in mind. A few examples follow:

☞ "What makes your company special in the field?"
☞ "What do you consider the hardest part of this position?"
☞ "Where are your greatest opportunities for growth?"
☞ "Do you know when you might need anything further from me?"

Leave discussion of terms for future conversations. Make a cordial, smooth exit.

Remember to Follow Up

Send a thank-you note. Employers surveyed by CareerBuilder.com in 2005 said it matters. About 15 percent said they would not hire someone who did not follow up with a thanks. And almost 33 percent would think less of a candidate. The form of the note does not much matter—if you know a manager's preference, use it. Otherwise, just be sure to follow up.

Winning an Offer

A job offer can feel like the culmination of a long and difficult struggle. So naturally, when you hear them, you may be tempted to jump at the offer. Don't. Once an employer wants you, he or she will usually give you a chance to consider the offer. This is the time to discuss terms of employment, such as vacation, overtime, and benefits. A little effort now can be well worth it in the future. Be sure to do a check of prevailing salaries for your field and area before signing on. Web sites for this include Payscale.com, Salary.com, and Salaryexpert.com. If you are thinking about asking for better or different terms from what the prospective employer offered, rest assured—that's how business gets done; and it may just burnish the positive impression you have already made.

Index

DATE			